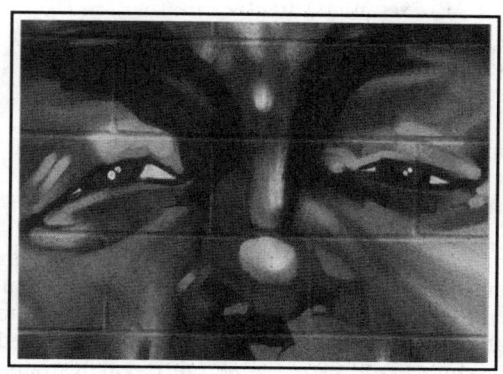

The Full Spectrum: Essays on Staff Diversity in Corrections

Carla J. Smalls, Editor

Lanham, Maryland
American Correctional Association

Mission of the American Correctional Association

The American Correctional Association provides a professional organization for all individuals and groups, both public and private, that share a common goal of improving the justice system.

American Correctional Association Staff

Charles J. Kehoe, President
James A. Gondles, Jr., CAE, Executive Director
Gabriella Daley Klatt, Director, Communications and Publications
Harry Wilhelm, Marketing Manager
Alice Heiserman, Manager of Publications and Research
Michael Kelly, Associate Editor
Dana M. Murray, Graphics and Production Manager
Joseph Fuller, II, Graphics and Production Associate
Cover design by Darlene Jones

Printed in the United States of America by Automated Graphic Systems, Inc., White Plains, MD.

This publication may be ordered from:
American Correctional Association
4380 Forbes Boulevard
Lanham, Maryland 20706-4322
1-800-222-5646

For information on publications and videos available from ACA, contact our worldwide web home page at: http://www.aca.org

ISBN 1-56991-210-6

Library of Congress Cataloging-in-Publication Data

The full spectrum : essays on staff diversity in corrections / Carla Smalls, editor.
    p. cm.
  Includes index.
  ISBN 1-56991-210-6 (pbk.)
Correctional personnel—United States. 2. Prisons—United States—Officials and employees. 3. Minorities—Employment—United States. 4. Diversity in the workplace. I.
  Smalls, Carla. II. American Correctional Association.

  HV9470.F85 2003
  365'.973'0683—dc22

2003062833

Table of Contents

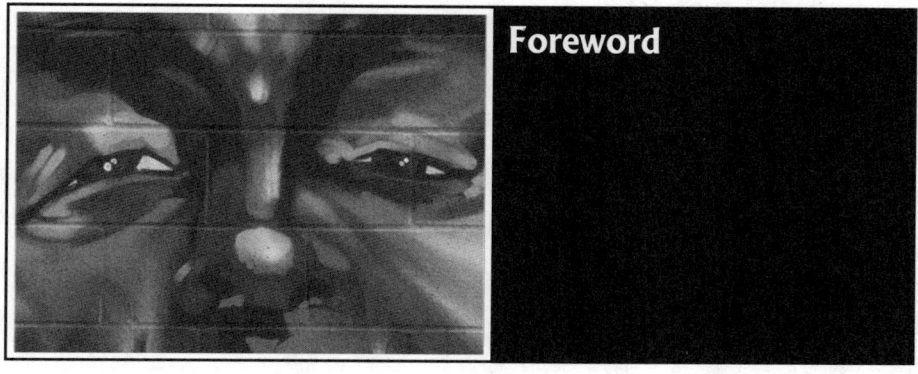

Foreword

W hen you next go to work, spend a few minutes looking around you at the other staff. How are you like them? How are you different? How many differences can you detect? Some of them are obvious — gender, age, race. Other differences are more subtle but meaningful such as differences in religion, culture or sexual orientation. ACA is pleased to offer this collection of essays on staff diversity issues in corrections. Carla Smalls, the editor of this collection, worked diligently to secure the writers and identify relevent topics.

This collection of essays by respected members of the field is a start towards better understanding. If we recognize and appreciate diversity, we can learn to work together better and accomplish more. Or, we may find that in ways that matter, we are more alike than we thought at first glance.

I hope that corrections professional at all levels will read these essays for their own professional growth and development and correctional trainers will use this book for in-service and pre-service training.

James A. Gondles, Jr., CAE
Executive Director
American Correctional Association

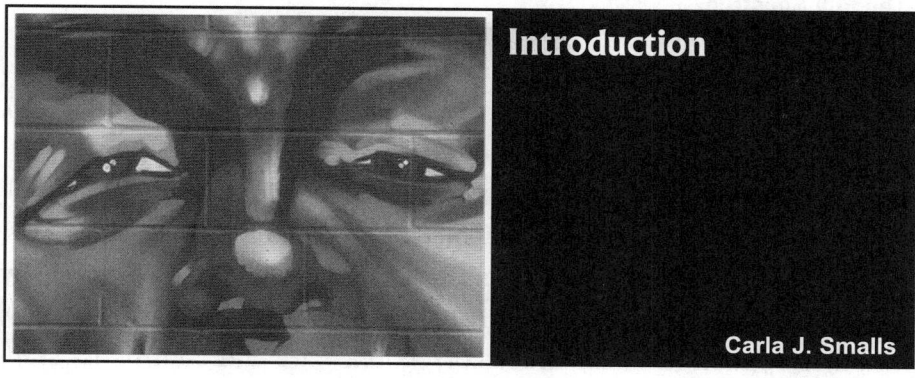

Introduction

Carla J. Smalls

The word "diversity" often means different things to people. The variety of meanings and interpretations illustrate the essence of diversity. This includes many points of view, many styles and approaches—all based on ideas reflective of diverse backgrounds and experiences. Usually a discussion of diversity focuses on primary dimensions of diversity such as race, gender, and ethnicity. Yet, these dimensions only reflect one component of diversity and are a part of a larger portrait of variety that includes secondary dimensions, such as religion, age, and communication style.

One may pose the question: Why is the American Correctional Association interested in an examination of diversity? A review of two documents that guide and direct the operation of the American Correctional Association address this question. In the Code of Ethics of the American Correctional Association, which was adopted in August 1975 at the 105th Congress of Correction and revised August 1994 at the 124th Congress of Correction, one of the principles states: "Members shall respect and protect the civil and legal rights of all individuals." And another states: "Members shall refrain from discriminating against any individual because of race, gender, creed, national origin, religious affiliation, age, disability, or any other type of prohibited discrimination." The Code of Ethics essentially states that we acknowledge differences in people, but these differences should not be used in a punitive or harmful manner against others.

In the Declaration of Principles approved by the Delegate Assembly at the Winter Conference in San Antonio, Texas, January 16, 2002, the first principle is humanity. The principle states in part: "Social order in a democratic society depends upon full recognition of individual worth and respect for the dignity of all members; therefore, laws, administrative policies and corrections practices must be governed by this principle and measured against standards of fairness and decency, whether applied to those under corrections care and control, its staff, crime victims or the general public." The Code of Ethics and the Declaration of Principles articulate the American Correctional Association's position on the value of diversity.

This book is a tangible demonstration of one way that the American Correctional Association manifests the lofty ideals written in the Code of Ethics and the Declaration of Principles. Each chapter was written by a criminal justice professional and presents a unique perspective on valuing diversity from that individual's vantage point. The book is written for all levels of correctional professionals with chapters of interest to entry-level and executive-management staff. You may not agree with all of the perspectives, but surely you will be challenged to think about how you value diversity.

And as you think, use the words of the following poem to guide you.

If You and I Should Differ
If you and I should differ
In our beliefs
In our philosophies
In our culture
In our appearances
In our understanding of things
In our individual worlds

We may come to realize it is not important
That we agree.
Nor is it important
That we create perfect harmony.

Only that we respect each other's right to be different.
Only that we respect each other's right to be heard.

The poem "If You and I Should Differ" was reprinted from the book, *Don't Quit, Inspirational Poetry*, by Mychal Wynn, copyright 1990, revised 1997, ISBN 1-880463-26-1. Reprint permission granted on March 3, 2003 from the publisher, Rising Sun Publishing, Inc. P.O. Box 70906, Marietta, GA 30007.

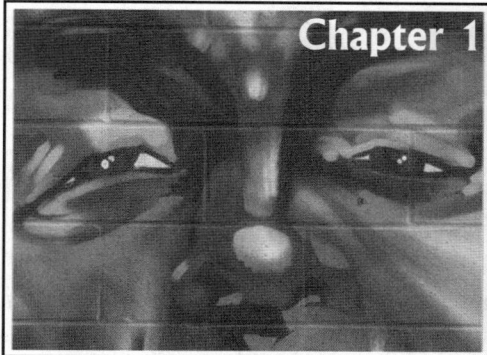

Chapter 1 Effective Communication Embraces Diversity

Linda Dillon
Chief Executive Officer/Consultant
Innovative Concepts
Springfield, Illinois

People across various cultures interact with others from varying backgrounds on an ongoing basis, especially in a correctional environment. Celebrating this diversity is a necessary component for an effective communication process. At times, we can recognize prejudices by the level of influence that affects our decisions. Our ethnicity, the influence from our contacts, and how we process it all makes us who we are. This can and often does become a life-long challenge of sorting the positive decisions and experiences from the negative ones. This process of sorting (which we often do without conscious effort) allows us to become effective communicators, but we can be more effective if we stop and analyze our communication and that of others.

At times, however, we are faced with a difficult challenge of cultural diversity. It raises questions and sets us off balance and we may experience feelings of inadequacy. Those times may occur when we observe two or more people try and communicate, but one is dressed differently or speaks a different language, and the other person just does not get it. That other person might be us. How do we handle situations such as this? The author observed two people trying to effectively communicate. One person was Spanish-speaking and the other English-speaking. The English-speaking person was yelling. The Spanish-speaking person, not understanding why he was being yelled at, was becoming frustrated and angry. The author interrupted this situation and asked the English-speaking person why he was speaking so loudly. He looks puzzled and said, "I wasn't speaking loudly." "You were," the author replied. He dropped his head saying he did not realize he was doing that. I told him that the gentleman spoke a different language, he was not hard of hearing.

One's lack of understanding of another's culture often may result in superficial and sarcastic expressions. When one makes frivolous comments or even shows a flagrant disregard for respecting others' differences, it reduces the person's credibility. The messages the diversity trainer sends out to the group may be just as important as the desired outcome. The trainer should provide a positive model that the learners may emulate.

Ask yourself: do you believe that your own perspective is the only real one and that anything that does not comfortably fit within it is a waste of time, just wrong, unworkable or irrelevant? J. Edgar Hoover once said that the only way anyone can become a good American is to act, dress, speak and perhaps look like what he thinks an American should look like. This concept, although archaic, still exists today. However, this concept is far removed from the actual reality. The reality is that Americans come in all forms and speak in a wide range of ways. How an individual views things—his or her perception—also must be considered in this sorting process because perception can be one's only reality.

As professionals, we encounter daily experiences in communities, various aspects of criminal justice, law enforcement, and corrections. We need to understand that we cannot expect everyone to act or speak the same way. We need to ask ourselves: Is there another way to see this issue or situation? Can we step into someone else's shoes and consider how she or he is viewing things? Does this make a difference in your final analysis of the issue? Our job and goal is to know how to understand and then address the many individual differences that staff and inmates bring. We can do this best by building teams within our respective disciplines to work together to come to common conclusions and ways of working together cooperatively. If we do not make this effort, we then become supporters and possibly enablers of problematic staff or coworkers.

When we are not prepared to use a positive approach in resolving situational conflicts and misunderstandings, several negative reactions set the stage for a reoccurrence of the problems. In these cases several things may happen:

- Productivity drops
- Isolation of staff occurs
- Suspicion and distrust among staff increases
- There is higher staff turnover
- The number of disgruntled employees increases
- The whole climate of the correctional institution changes

Yet, it need not be this way.

Individuals need to assess how much they already know and how well they really communicate with others from a background different from theirs. Rather than get frustrated about their inability to communicate, they should consider that they are at the beginning of their learning and have an opportunity to gain greater insight into themselves and others, and by doing so have a greater opportunity to be understood.

The first stage is understanding yourself. Ask yourself: When I speak, what am I saying? What do I mean? Am I concerned with honorable intentions? Do I understand communicating is a process of giving and receiving information.

More than fifteen years ago, this author moved to Canton, a small rural town in central Illinois, to be assistant warden of programs for a

1,200-bed, medium-security facilities with an all male population. The population of the town consisted of about 98 percent nonminorities and 1 percent African-Americans.

Opening a newly built prison involves a very long work day. The goal is to get the prison open and up and running within the time constraints identified. During this particular week, the author had worked unusually long hours. Having worked ten consecutive days for ten and sixteen hours, this particular Friday was her reprieve. Leaving at 4:00 PM, she already had planned her evening and the entire weekend: to eat and *SLEEP*. She was covering each moment in her mind as she was driving home. She had to make one quick stop by the grocery store to pick up a loaf of bread and orange juice. This was to be an in-and-out quick trip, then home and to bed! No pagers, no phone calls, no visitors, no small talk with the neighbors. And when she got to the grocery store, she pictured no standing in the long lines, absolutely nothing to keep her from her queen-size supreme firm bed.

She pulled into the angled parking space. As her eyes moved to the left, she noticed an older robust, burly white gentleman seated on a sidewalk bench. He was dressed in a pair of overalls, only one strap hooked in place. He looked to be in his mid-eighties, needed a shave, had ruffled golden gray hair and was not very attractive. His boots were worn and scuffed, a discolored grayish tan. Neither boot was laced as he sat in a swayed but appealingly relaxed and confident position. He looked or rather stared at the author for an unusually long time.

She stepped out of her assigned "state vehicle" and walked toward the entrance of the grocery store. It was in the direct pathway of the senior gentleman. He watched every step she made, his eyes moving in a type of rhythm, as if he were investigating her, beginning with the shoes on her feet all the way up her body to the hair on her head, glancing now and then at the state vehicle. As she drew near, many things were going through her mind. She was tired and did not feel like dealing with any "drama." As she approached him, each looked at one another. Finally, she was in front of him. "Good afternoon," she said. He quickly blurted out, "So you're the colored gal that works out at the prison?" She hesitated for just a second but replied "Yes, sir." He then asked, "Aren't you scared?" She thought to herself, how ironic that he was concerned for her. But she responded softly, "No, there are other female employees who worked at the prison and are black, Mexican, and white."

The author took this "opportunity" to explain the offender classification process and what level of security offenders would be housed at this prison. He appeared to be so pleased with the conversation that he called out to one of the store owner's to come over and meet her or as he said in a whisper "the nice black lady," all the time glancing at me for my approval. She smiled, shaking her head in agreement. The story does not stop there, for she later learned that this old gentleman was a pillar of the community who was extremely influential. He was supportive of her and shared this with the community, always introducing her after that, as "the nice black lady."

Imagine how the ending would have occurred had her comments been different with the gentleman's statement "So you're the colored gal that works out at the prison." Had she said something flippant, sarcastic, rude, or even disrespectful, neither would have understood the other and resentment would have grown. Instead, she continued the dialog, and she was afforded the opportunity to educate and orient this person from a different generation and culture. A popular quote speaks of profound truth and respect. "To understand another human being you must gain insight into the conditions which made him what he is."

As professionals, it behooves us to look at situations and determine what the desired outcome should be before thinking about the resolution. How can you do this? As we study and examine variables and factors that would allow us to play worst-case scenarios on the tape recorders of our mind, we must identify the value of differences and clarify or create a common understanding. The next step is to create and develop strategies that cause positive impacts in relationships and our work environments.

The book, *Beyond Race and Gender: Unleashing the Power of Your Total Work Force by Managing Diversity* (1992, Amacom) by R. Roosevelt Thomas, Jr. gives an excellent summary and comparative analysis on the areas of affirmative action, including valuing differences and managing diver-sity. One of the strengths of this book is how it discusses applying communication and recognizing that diversity plays a highly important role in this process—especially when one desires to be an effective communicator. Understanding, respecting, and valuing differences among the persons we serve and work with can only support us in our many capacities as we interface with others in our day-to-day challenges.

Self-development begins with cultivating and increasing self-awareness through educating oneself on the facts and myths of one's own culture and that of others and seeing how you can learn to value the differences between them. Then, one must practice what one has learned. The following example illustrates this principle. A correctional officer's and offender's miscommunication resulted in the misunderstanding of the offender's failure to attend his religious prayer service. The author entered one of the facility's housing unit foyers, where an offender and a correctional officer were engaged in an argument. As she approached them, they turned to watch her and immediately began to explain their versions of what the problem was. The offender was yelling, "I want his job. He denied me my religious rights. I'm going to sue him. He kept me from attending jumar." The correctional officer explained, "The offender asked me if they were holding jumar today, so I checked the gym schedule. It wasn't on there so I told him 'no'." She asked the officer why he checked the gym schedule. He said he thought *jumar* was some type of intramural game and that was why he checked that list.

The offender then proceeded to explain that it is the officer's responsibility to know what *jumar* was. The author interrupted the offender asking him how this officer would know that. Given the location of the prison and knowing the officer's background, the author found it highly unlikely that the officer would have known what the offender was talking about. As the dialog continued, the officer, after learning that jumar was a Muslim prayer service, stated from that point on he would check every list on the clipboard when asked about the activities in the institution. And the offender indicated that when he went to check to confirm what activities would be taking place, he would provide more information such as the *jumar* prayer service, clueing the officer in so he could check the chapel list. Both agreed and apologized for any misunderstanding and all was resolved.

As the example illustrates, it is important to confirm the intentions of the sender's initial statement or message. Are you interpreting the message in the same way that it is sent? Do you accept and respect the words of the speaker? This is the key to successful communication. When you approach anyone with the intentions of communicating, your expectations are simple. You expect the person or persons to accept you as an equal human being.

You also expect to be accepted with respect and given the opportunity to be heard and understood. You have the right to have your expressions valued, because your thoughts and words are important. Ask yourself, do you allow the person who approaches you the same latitude? Does the other person have the same learning style as you do? Can he or she understand what you are saying in the way you intended? Can the individual respond in an appropriate way? Will this response be different from what you might expect from someone of the same ethnic background as you? By taking into account the individual's ethnicity, one can appreciate and value differences. Part of becoming or maintaining the ability of being an effective communicator includes, but is not limited to, the constant review of one's own tolerance of ambiguity or situations that are not clear to you.

How are you at the "change process"? Do you struggle when you have to communicate with a new or different person? Or, are you able to adjust and modify your expectations based on the individual? A second personal attribute to be considered is cognitive and behavioral flexibility. How would you introduce or present yourself to someone whose ethnicity was different from yours? At work, within the community or in other environments, what would you say? Better yet, what choice of words would you use and why? Do you stop to consider one's learning styles or diverse needs? Or are you totally consumed with the person interfacing with you in a one-way dialog?

Taking the next step requires our examination of "personal self-awareness." One's sense of identity is a perception that others see. But what do we allow them to see? Has our identity been defined? By whom? Do we portray a strong sense of who we are? Are we confident and self-assured in our actions? Are we open and honest in our relationships, or do we selectively choose in which relationships we are open and honest?

If we are guilty of not being open or honest in all our relationships, for what reasons do we make these specific choices? Following this examination automatically forces us to initiate an analysis of "cultural self-awareness." Here we look at how we became who we are. Many people never get to this point in their lives. They will walk through their entire lives not realizing or caring to consider how they developed their value systems.

Look at the following questions and think about your answers:

- How many of your cultural norms were adapted from other cultural orientations?
- How much of your own uniqueness is sustained through the patterns of behavior and beliefs that you gained from relatives?
- What patterns of behavior and beliefs did you gain from friends?
- What were those patterns of behavior and beliefs that you gained from coworkers?
- What is the influence of your religion on your patterns of behavior and belief?
- What is the result of your schooling on your patterns of behavior and belief?

What people bring to us, what we bring to people, and what we expect of ourselves sets the tone for how we choose to interface with each person with whom we come in contact. Patience and commitment work hand and hand in the development of respect. This allows the partners in the communication process to fully have the opportunity to understand the message. Know that each of us has our own learning styles. Recognize that each time we speak, we can demonstrate our self-enthusiasm and make it easier for others to communicate effectively with us.

A second component of effective communication is tolerance of differences. You can learn about people from listening to them and from reading. Reading can bring new depths of understanding. Developing a sense of humor towards yourself is important so that when you make mistakes about something cultural, you can learn to laugh at yourself and not at the other person. Developing a sense of humility and a real respect for the true complexities of one's own culture, ethnicity, and diversity also are important ways that we can deal with situations in which others have a different background or orientation than we do. As we develop in this way, we gain a new sense of empathy and experience self-growth.

Anthony T. Browder, in *The Declaration of Innocence: The Nile Valley's Contributions to Civilization* (1992, Institute of Karmic Guidance) offers some guidance that we can use as a checklist for our own communication:

- I have not spoken lies.
- I have not dealt deceitfully.
- I have not set my lips in motion (against any man [or woman]).
- I have not stirred up strife.
- I have not judged hastily.
- I have not spoken scornfully.
- I have not stopped my ears against the words of Right and Truth.

As you read these words, rate your degree of compliance.

Communicating respectfully with each person (other staff and inmates) and others in other areas of our life is an opportunity to enhance who we are—gaining additional insights not only of the other person, but of ourselves. It allows an opportunity for open and honest communication. It confirms our reason and ability to engage in interpersonal sensitivity. And it affords us that exciting challenge to be introduced to the variety of individuals and cultures that may offer insights and perceptions that allow us to embrace life more fully.

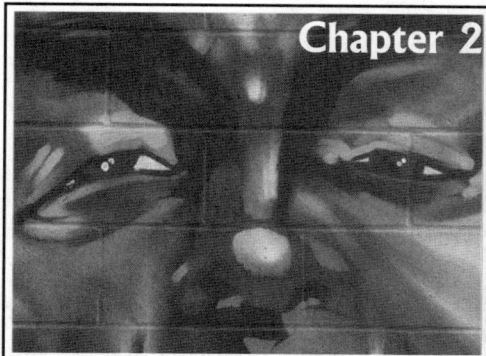

Chapter 2 Age Diversity in Corrections

William "Bill" Sturgeon, President
Institute for Adult Education
and Training
Pittsfield, Massachusetts

At the beginning of this new millennium, age diversity in the field of corrections has taken on a life of its own. One reason for this is because the baby boomers are fast approaching the age when many of them will be eligible for retirement. Another reason may be because laws have changed permitting adjudicated juveniles to be incarcerated in adult prisons. Thus, for many reasons, the topic of age diversity in the field of corrections has a multitude of issues associated with it. Because corrections is a people business, characteristics such as age represent significant managerial and operational issues that correctional leaders and staff need to consider.

One of the things that makes corrections such a unique career field is the way it has bridged many diversity issues. When it comes to its employees, corrections for at least the past thirty years has made a significant effort to generate an atmosphere of openness to all people —regardless of age, color, gender, religion, and ethic origin. To some groups, specifically, women and people of color, this openness came slowly and not without its struggles, but the reality is—it did come.

When it comes to age diversity, some people think it only applies to older workers. It also applies to inmates and their diverse needs and ages. Thus, age diversity is not simply about older people in the work-force or in prisons. Age diversity means recognizing that staff of all ages have something to contribute. It is about ensuring that all have the opportunity to realize their potential—no matter if they are young or old. "The older worker should not be dismissed as being 'out of touch,' the younger worker should not be dismissed as 'too inexperienced,' and the workers in-between should not be dismissed as having 'gone as far as they can go'" (Cabinet Office, United Kingdom, 2003).

Generalizing about groups of people by national origin, color, or age is wrong. Yet, it is still done. However, it is a trap that agencies must be aware of when dealing with any diversity issue. Ensuring diversity in the workplace should go beyond fulfilling quotas or ratios, the "civil rights" idea of diversity. It should be based on basic "human rights," where capable people are insured an opportunity for employment.

Age diversity is something that is very rarely spotlighted as one of the main diversity areas. Yet, age diversity in corrections has proven to be an important element in the operation of a correctional agency. The author believes that employing people of various ages gives correctional agencies the ability to adapt and deliver a well-rounded approach to inmate/client management. The more experienced staff has the "on the job" maturity to be able to identify changing dynamics and to adjust the operation to meet these changes. The younger less experienced bring with them a positive "can do" spirit. Their youth permits them to challenge the old operational paradigms. This interaction among age groups occurs within the confines of a correctional environment. Correctional leaders need to be well rounded so they can remain flexible to address the continuously changing human dynamics of both the inmates and the staff.

As an example of this, several states have established youthful offender programs to manage the increase in adjudicated juveniles sentenced as adults to adult institutions. This has required a great deal of flexibility in housing arrangements, programming, staff training, and most importantly, staffing. Anecdotal evidence appears to reinforce the concept of a successful program resulting from having a combination of staff that is made up of people of various age groups. Older staff who had years of correctional experience demonstrate the ability to adapt to meet the unique demands of youthful offenders incarcerated in adult facilities. Younger correctional employees with little experience demonstrate the ability to understand the youthful offenders' jargon and needs and have the energy and vitality to keep up with them. The younger staff members greatly assisted the older staff in understanding the differences in dealing with this inmate population.

As with other diversity issues, age diversity also has stereotypes. The age diversity stereotypes in corrections can be similar to the ones listed below.

Group One—Those with a Great Deal of Experience

Of course, not all people from any age group fit all the stereotypes—no more than all people from any sexual, racial, or ethnic group fit all the stereotypes. However, for argument's sake, we will assume that Group One has a great deal of correctional experience, and the following characteristics:

- Ages range between thirty-eight and fifty-six years old
- Has a significant number of years on the job
- Has experienced considerable progression/promotions up the "career ladder" to senior levels of supervision and management
- Has been involved in a number of different and demanding workplace activities at many levels
- Has developed certain behaviors, skills, knowledge, and abilities
- Has many years (fifteen plus) of longevity in the workplace environment
- Has received a great deal of workplace training
- Is looking more toward retirement than advancement/or transferring
- Has climbed most of the "career ladder"
- May be more content with the workplace environment and situation and demonstrates some resistance to change
- Is very content with the status quo

Group Two—Those with Some Experience

Make the assumption that Group Two has some correctional experience, and has these characteristics:

- Ages range between twenty-nine and thirty-seven years old
- Has some years on the job
- Has some progression/promotions up the "career ladder" to entry-level management and mid-level supervision
- Has been involved in some different and demanding workplace activities at levels equal to their position with the agency
- Is developing certain behaviors, skills, knowledge, and abilities
- Has some years (five-to-fourteen years) of longevity in the workplace
  - Has received some training
- Is looking forward to further advancements/transfers
- Is still climbing the "career ladder"
- Wants to change things to meet their needs and desires. They are not content with the status quo and are looking for change.

Group Three—Those with Very Little Experience

Make the assumption that the Group Three has very little correctional experience, and has the following characteristics:

- Ages range between nineteen and twenty-eight years old
- Does not have a lot of time on the job
- Has little to no progression/promotions up the "career ladder"
- Has been involved in very few different and demanding workplace activities
- Is still deciding on what behaviors, skills, knowledge, and abilities they will need
- Has less than five years on the job

- Has only received entry-level training
- Is trying to figure out the "career ladder"
- Does not know if things should change or remain the same

All too often people get caught up in trying to validate the characteristics of each group rather than trying to dispel them. Although some of the characteristics listed above may have some validity, they are, for the most part, just stereotypical characteristics used to describe people who work in corrections.

A predominance of white males in their late forties to mid-fifties dominate high-level positions. But with the exodus of the baby boomer generation, it is reasonable to expect that when these people retire, many of these positions will be filled by women, people of color, and of course, younger individuals. These groups will bring with them, into management positions, their experiences, knowledge, and skills developed in different paradigms than those of the baby boomer white male. Their ways of doing things may disturb the status quo and put a halt to the "we have always done it that way" answers.

The reality is that each age group brings to the correctional environment its own contributions and personality. How many have known someone with a great deal of time on the job but who has not contributed anything substantial for several years. As the old saying goes, ""Mr. X has one year of experience twenty times." Similarly, some people have very little experience but greatly contribute daily to the operations of the agency.

Where the field of corrections differs from some other career fields is that to fulfill its mission, it has to mix staff from different age groups together in a specialized "closed" environment to manage an inmate population as age diversified as the staff. Unlike a manufacturing plant where there are management, supervisors, and line staff, and the "product," in corrections the "product" is the inmate population that can and often does change daily. Throughout the years, corrections has demonstrated its ability to adapt to meet the needs of each age group (generation). When the inmate population started to get older and needed a different type of management, corrections had the foresight to start to develop special management methods and techniques for dealing with geriatric inmates. Another example of corrections' ability to adapt to the changing inmate demographics is that during the influx of youthful offenders (adjudicated juveniles—those individuals under the age of majority) many states established special programs to manage this population.

More than other career fields, corrections attempts to accommodate the needs of all age groups, as well as any bureaucracy that is a twenty-four/seven operation can. This is unlike other career fields that try to "construct a workplace based on a single generation's expectations of benefits and conditions" (Gomolski, 2001). During the high technology boom, the press was filled with dot.com companies that boasted that they did not have anyone older than their mid-twenties.

Because the field of corrections has experienced unprecedented growth over the past twenty years, the need for more staff aided in breaking down many of the diversity roadblocks. This growth in corrections has forced the field to open its doors to people of all ages to fill the tremendous and seemingly never-ending demand for employees. This "open door/open age" effort has aided the field of corrections in overcoming the multitude of generational issues that have caused other career fields such difficulties. Having people of all ages join the correctional workforce in such a short period of time has further helped discredit many stereotypes.

The make-up of today's correctional staff is constantly changing. It is not uncommon to see people who have joined the correctional workforce in their forties to start a second career along with young people who are just joining the fulltime workforce. Another phenomenon that cannot be overlooked is the growth of private corrections. Public corrections is losing people of all ages to private corrections. Many experienced people are leaving correctional agencies to become private consultants. The field of corrections has gone from the stepchild of the criminal justice community to one of the nation's primary employers, both in the private and public sector. Corrections is a career field that requires the talents and skills of people from every age group to fulfill its missions.

New correctional employees represent people of different ages and generations, all of whom bring with them a variety of skills, knowledge, experiences, and work habits they have learned in other career fields, such as law enforcement, the military, and construction. There are also people joining the correctional workforce right out of college, and they bring with them youth and knowledge. In most cases, all of these people desire to climb the career ladder.

Few people grew up saying, "I want to work in corrections." Many of the people who work in corrections, the author of this article included, have come from other career fields. They brought with them all the skills, knowledge, and experiences that they gained in those other career fields and, in some cases, have, been able to use them in corrections. People from the military and law enforcement brought with them the discipline of those agencies while those from the construction trades brought with them the hard work ethic associated with these trades.

The wide variety of experience, and the age diversity of the people who work in today's corrections, have assisted corrections in its ability to evaluate, re-evaluate, and adjust its responses to issues such as: inmate crowding, gang proliferation, unprecedented new prison/jail construction, staffing shortages, HIV/AIDS, the aging inmate population, longer sentences, increased case loads in parole and probation departments, and the introduction of adjudicated juvenile offenders into adult prisons.

In today's correctional work environment, diversity in general and age specifically, has become one of the anchors. There are few career fields where there is such an age diverse group of employees as in corrections. This may be because some of the retirement plans require people to work a great number of years before they can collect their full pension. For some people, corrections is a second career, and there are women who have reentered the workforce after their children have entered school. Correctional employees, without question, truly represent a mosaic of American society.

Baby Boomers

Like all career fields, the field of corrections soon will be facing what could be a serious crisis to its age diversity, "experiential brain drain." Over the next few years, the "Baby Boomers" will be retiring en masse, taking with them their knowledge and experience. The extent of the baby boomers' exodus from the work place is going to result in a significant decrease in age diversity. Below are two samples from a survey conducted by the author in 2001:

Sample One

More than 21 percent of one agency's senior management (agency head, deputy agency heads, and chief administrators) currently are eligible for retirement, while 32.4 percent of the agency's senior field/institutional staff currently are eligible for retirement.

Sample Two

About 58 percent of another agency's senior management are currently eligible for retirement, and 40 percent of the agency's senior field/institutional staff currently are eligible for retirement.

As these samples illustrate, every managerial and operational area of corrections will be affected by the loss of the baby boomer generation. If the baby boomers left at a slower pace, agencies could prepare for this type of loss. It is the rapid loss of the baby boomers from the workforce that can have adverse affects on the management and operations of an agency unless the agency plans for such a loss.

The consistency of staff in a correctional environment has proven through the years to be a key component to inmate management and agency stability. The retirement of the baby boomers will affect correctional agencies at every level and in every department. Many of the baby boomers currently hold positions in upper-level management, mid-management, and supervision. They are policymakers, operational directors—and they are senior people. Their loss from these positions will have a ripple effect across agencies.

Those agencies that wish to be proactive are moving now to help fill the void that will be created by the rapid loss of the baby boomers. This is done by identifying where and exactly when the losses will take place. Once the extent of the losses are determined and top-level staff know where exactly the losses will be, a training process to prepare people to take over these vacated positions must be implemented. Some of this training should be to ensure that those people who will be moving up the career ladder have the formal education necessary and/or required to fill the vacated positions. Another part of the process, and possibly the most difficult, is designing training programs where those people who will be filling these positions have an opportunity to gain "real life" work experience by working with the people who they will succeed.

These training programs must be focused, in that they prepare people of all ages to assume positions of responsibility throughout an agency. These training programs should be a combination of classroom instruction, mentoring, shadowing, and practical experience.

Classroom Instruction

Classroom instruction should consist of a variety of supervisory and management courses that are geared specifically toward public sector human services/criminal justice agencies. There should be courses that develop the knowledge and skills in areas such as:

- Budget development/management
- Policy development
- Human resources/labor relations
- Management/supervisory techniques

- Public/media relations
- Understanding the legislative process

Mentoring

Mentoring programs must be structured and intense. Performance in such programs also should be part of the mentors' performance evaluation. Mentoring programs should work at developing people and be somewhat competitive. People selected to become part of the mentoring process should be selected from a pool of employees who want to be part of a mentoring program. The goals and objectives of a mentoring program should be explained to them prior to their entering the program. Mentors should be selected from personnel who the administration feels are very proficient in their positions. There are several good mentoring programs available from the National Institute of Corrections Information Center (www.nicic.org).

Shadowing

A shadowing program must permit the complete accessibility to the person(s) being shadowed. Participants must be able to actually view the persons being shadowed in the performance of their duties. Most importantly, the persons being shadowed should leave a portion of their day open for questions from the participants. The goals and objectives of the shadowing program should stress the process of performing the duties and tasks associated with specific positions. Included in the shadowing program should be those subtle nuances associated with performing the duties and tasks associated with specific positions, nuances such as what the short- and long-range demands of a new program may have on the agency's budget or the importance of developing an open line of communication with the line staff.

As mentioned previously, filling upper-level management positions will have a ripple effect on the entire agency. This means that not only should an agency have a training plan for those who will be filling upper-level management positions, but it must also must have a plan for training people who will be filling their positions. These programs should be centered on line-level supervision and entry-level management programs. The American Correctional Association and the National Institute of Corrections have training programs that can help agencies meet these demands. These training programs are as important as those for upper-level management because people in these positions are the people who have day-to-day contact with the inmate population and are responsible for carrying out agency policies and procedures.

Anecdotal demographics of the people who will be moving up to fill these vacant supervisory and entry-level positions indicate that they will be younger (non-baby boomers) than those leaving those positions and may not have a great deal of work experience. They, however, may have the same or more education than some of the people they are replacing. Given this anecdotal evidence, training programs should be centered on the practicality of job performance rather than philosophy.

The programs discussed are examples of what agencies can do to help prepare people to replace the retiring baby boomers. Corrections, however, must rethink its entire staff training initiatives. Staff training cannot be a mechanical process of basic, annual, and some specialty training. It will have to be more focused on staff career development. Preparing people to climb the career ladder will become a main tenet of modern day correctional training. The American Correctional Association has developed a series of courses to assist people in becoming correctional professionals, including online training.

Correctional training will have to develop training that meets the needs and desires of the generations already in the workplace and the new generations coming into the workplace. There need to be modern training approaches that encourage more interactive and high tech training methods. Unlike baby boomers, generation X and Y are very comfortable with using computers and other interactive training aids to fulfill their training needs. Staff from every level and discipline should be involved with identifying the training needs of an agency.

No longer can corrections wait until a person leaves to fill the position. Every effort should be made to have a period of time for the outgoing person to have an opportunity to work with the incoming person. Experience is something that is very difficult to impart. However, it is something that the agencies will have to try to do. The baby boomers have experienced a great many changes such as crowding, gangs, riots, and major disturbances in corrections and have learned how to overcome them. To let them retire without attempting to retain some of that "real life" experience would be unfair to those who will be replacing them.

Each age group (generation) has its own knowledge, skills, experiences, and cultural uniqueness that it brings to the work environment. Cultural uniqueness can be anything from type of music they enjoy, to openness to technology, their work ethic, their job loyalty, or their habits of reading the newspaper. A number of people in their twenties, thirties, and forties read the newspaper online. As history has proven, each generation makes changes in the way things are done. These changes are made because of their beliefs, available technology, societal demands, political intervention, and financial resources. A simple example can be the replacing of single-key cell doors with electro-mechanical sliding cell doors. As a result of the confluence of all these factors, the impact of the baby boomer brain drain phenomenon can and will have tremendous influences on the field of corrections, both positive and negative.

Positive Effects

-   The potential for promotion of younger staff up the career ladder of corrections
-   Members of a new generation(s) will be assuming different roles and control of the agencies

- The possibility of changes in the operations of the agency
- Enthusiasm for the newness and change (by some)

Negative Effects

- The rapid loss of experienced personnel (loss of the agency's history)
- The possibility of making operational and management mistakes during the "learning curve" process of the newly promoted
- Too much change, too fast
- Too much change without the work experience to assess the short- and long-term effects

Regardless of the positive or negative effects, the reality is that the baby boomers will be gone soon and another generation will take the helm. "When a paradigm shifts, everyone goes back to zero" (Barker, 1992). The correctional management paradigm has started to shift. Agencies that prepare for this paradigm shift by developing a comprehensive training plan will make the transition better than those that do not have a plan.

When looking at age diversity in the workplace, one also must look at unions. Unions, like agencies, will have to understand the needs and characteristics of different age groups that make up their membership. Younger union members needs may differ significantly from those of the baby boomers. Progressive agencies and unions should work together in developing the new work environment.

A great deal has been written about Generation X. One characteristic about Generation X that should concern correctional agencies is the prediction that members of this generation will be changing careers from five to seven or more times during their working years. Also, Generation X people want direct input into their careers. They want to know what plans agencies have for them. Possibly, this prediction of job changing could be reduced by agencies directly involving the people of this generation in developing their own career plans and planning training activities for their agencies.

Agencies should view age diversity as the opportunity to incorporate the skills, knowledge, uniqueness, and experience of people from every generation, and respect the contributions they make. Corrections always has modified itself to meet the demand placed on it by society by incorporating the ingenuity of its staff which always has been made up of people of all ages.

Inmates

Another unique area of age diversity in corrections is that of the inmates. Unlike many other career fields, corrections always has to be aware of the inmates and their issues and needs. Just as the staff is made of up of people from every generation, so too is the inmate population. Those who have worked in the field of corrections since the 1980s have seen inmate populations soar. The field of corrections went from a relatively stable inmate population to where each year inmate growth surpassed the previous year's growth.

At one point, inmate populations grew so fast that they outgrew the capacity of existing facilities, which caused growth in the construction of new jails and prisons. To add to the crowding problem of the 1980s and 1990s, many states changed their sentencing policies and parole and probation operations.

A number of states changed their sentencing laws (truth in sentencing/three strikes, and so forth) to require inmates to serve a longer duration of their sentences before they would be eligible for parole. Additionally, states revised their juvenile laws to allow for juveniles to be charged and tried as adults and sentenced to adult prisons. These and other initiatives resulted in inmates coming to prisons younger, serving more time and, thereby, getting older in prison. It would be safe to say that with the entry of youthful offenders (adjudicated juveniles), America's prisons incarcerate people from almost every generation. Today's prisons incarcerate the old and the young.

They include the following:

- The Greatest Generation (those born before 1946)
- The Baby Boomers (those born between 1946 - 1964)
- Generation X and Y (those born after 1964)

Dealing with the needs of these various generations now being confined in a correctional environment requires a workforce that is flexible, mature, and diverse.

Many correctional agencies are finding out that today's younger inmates (Generation X and Y) are coming into prisons without the skills that the inmates of the past (Greatest Generation and Baby Boomers) have had. For years, correctional budgets have been kept down because they employed inmates to help with the routine maintenance of the institutions. Inmates possessed a variety of skills. They included: electricians, carpenters, plumbers, painters, and so forth. Also, the educational needs of the younger inmates are more dramatic. Many of them are still operating at the elementary level. These generational differences will have a financial impact on correctional operations.

Youthful offenders (adjudicated juveniles) present very serious generational issues to corrections agencies (Glick and Sturgeon, 2001). They have to be housed separately from adult inmates, and they require additional educational programs and specially trained staff. Correctional personnel assigned to work with youthful offenders say that they are a very demanding population. Because of their immaturity, they have a difficult time adjusting to prison routine. Some of these youthful offenders will spend a majority of their lives incarcerated.

These youthful offenders represent one end of the inmate population, while elderly (geriatric) inmates represent the other. The elderly inmates require specialized management just as the youthful offenders do. As inmates grow older, they demand more medical attention and medicine. Their senses become dulled. They become very set in their ways and are very reluctant to change. They also can become victims to the predators of the inmate population.

What seems to be happening is that there is a "natural age divide" among the inmates. There are three distinct major groups: the youthful offender, the middle-aged offender, and the older offender, with the middle-aged offenders rapidly catching up to the older offenders. The time may come when some prisons will have older inmate populations whose medication/medical budgets will rival their security budgets.

Society

Politicians have found that public safety is a good platform to campaign from and one in which the public is interested. Because of this, they began to change laws that had a direct effect on the inmate population and staffing. These changes have required correctional agencies to be able to house more inmates, from diverse backgrounds and ages, for much longer periods of time. To try to comprehend the complexity of this task, imagine having several people who you know (grandmother, grandfather, mother, father, brothers, sisters, cousins, neighbors, and a class of high school seniors) all housed together in your house. Consider that they are fully dependent on you for everything from what they eat to what they watch on television or listen to on the radio. In reality, that is what today's correctional environment is like. In almost every prison, there are people who represent every age group, race, origin, and religion and they are housed together for periods of time ranging from a few months to life.

This short discussion about age diversity may be different from the normal statistical and politically correct discussions. The author's goal is to have you understand how the field of corrections cannot operate effectively with people from only one age group/generation. Corrections has opened its doors, sometimes slowly, to people of color and women, so that its staff now is more representative of American society. Corrections is in the process of incorporating all people of every age into the fabric of its management and operations.

The author is now in his mid-fifties, but as he looks back, he remembers his own age diversity journey in corrections. He remembered his twenties, trying to decide what would be the fastest way to climb the career ladder and gain more experience. Then, in his thirties, he gained status, experience, and responsibility, and a clearer vision of where he wanted to go and how to get there. In his forties, he had achieved significant status and experience and had a clear vision of where he wanted to be and how. During each one of those decades, he has had the opportunity to witness corrections evolve into the rewarding career field it is today.

Age diversity in the field of corrections is here to stay. Just as the inmate population grows older, so too does the staff. As one generation leaves the workplace, another will take its place. The goals for agencies with regard to age diversity should be the following:

1. Encourage your experienced staff to stay until their replacement can be trained.
2. Create a workplace environment where the needs and issues of each generation are considered and respected.
3. Create a workplace environment that encourages and rewards input from all ages.
4. Create a workplace environment that actively addresses turnover.
5. Create training programs that permit people to develop their careers, meet the needs and desires of workers regardless of generation, and where the staff has input into the staff training program.
6. Create mentoring and shadowing programs where agency leaders help employees to assume supervisory and managerial positions.
7. Regard age diversity not from a legal perspective, but from a human rights perspective.

As states and agencies try to reduce their personnel budgets, they are offering early retirement or "golden parachutes" to many of their senior employees. Although this may be a method for reducing budgets, the side effects of this will have a direct influence on the age diversity and experiential factor of the agency. People who will be eligible for these early-retirement offers are the very same people who have dedicated a number of years to an agency. Their ages can span from late forties to late fifties, and their years of service are often in excess of twenty years. Very often these people hold positions of authority and responsibility within their agencies. States and agencies which are considering this budget-cutting strategy need to closely assess what the "overall" short- and long-term effects will be on the management and operations of their agencies—including the ripple effect and the upheaval that will occur for months to come.

The future of corrections promises to be challenging and exciting. To meet these new challenges, corrections will have to maintain its diversified workforce. There always will be a need for those who have the wisdom of years and for those whose youth inspires all. Unlike other diversity issues, everyone will experience age diversity.

References

Cabinet Office, United Kingdom. 2003. *Age: Diversity. Civil Service Policy.* February 21,2002 Available at www.diversity-whatworks.gov.uk/age/ policy.asphtm.

Barker, Joel Arthur. 1992. *Future Edge.* New York: William Morrow.

Glick, Barry and William Sturgeon. 2001. *Recess Is Over: A Handbook For Managing Youthful Offenders In Adult Systems.* Lanham, Maryland: American Correctional Association. Lanham, Maryland.

Gomolski, Barbara. 2001. Managing Age Diversity in the Workplace. *Computerworld.* February 13. Available at, www.computerworld.com/cwi/story/0,1199,NAV64_STO 57654,00.html.

Losyk, Bob. 1997. *Managing a Changing Workforce: Achieving Outstanding Service with Today's Employees.* Davie, Florida: Workplace Trends Publishing Company.

Raines, Claire. 1997. *Beyond Generation X: A Practical Guide for Managers*. Menlo Park, California: Crisp Publications.

Tapscott, Don.1998. *Growing Up Digital: The Rise of the Net Generation*. New York: McGraw-Hill.

Thau, Richard D. and Jay S. Heflin. 1997. *Generations Apart: Xers vs. Boomers vs. the Elderly*. Amherst, New York: Prometheus Books.

Tulgan, Bruce. 1997. *The Manager's Pocket Guide to Generation X.* HRD Press, Amherst, Massachusetts: HRD Press.

———— 1998. *Managing Generation X: Bringing Out the Best in Young Talent*. Santa Monica, California: Merritt Publishing.

———— 1998. *Recruiting the Workforce of the Future*. Amherst, Massachusetts: HRD Press.

————. 1999. *FAST Feedback TM, 2nd Edition*. Amherst, Massachusetts: HRD Press.

Woodward, Nancy Hatch. 1999. The Coming of X Managers. *HR Magazine*. March.

Watters, Steve and Debi Davis. 1997. *Generation X: Unplugged*. NeoPolitique, Regent University's Robertson School of Government.

Zemke, Ron, Claire Raines, and Bob Filipczak. 2000. *Generations at Work: Managing the Clash of Veterans, Boomers, Xers and Nexters in Your Workplace*. New York: AMACOM.

Zill, Nicholas and John Robin. 1995. The Generation X Difference. *American Demographics*. April.

Chapter 3 Generational Implications of Cross-cultural Communication

Bob Crouch
Correctional Training Instructor
North Carolina Department
of Corrections
Apex, North Carolina

Introduction

In your professional environment, you may be interacting with people from backgrounds and cultures different from your own. We are born with primary dimensions of diversity; they are the core of our being. They include our age, race, ethnicity, gender, sexual orientation, and physical abilities or qualities. These qualities refer to physical characteristics inherent to human beings, such as height—being short or tall—development disabilities, and other characteristics that are an immutable part of our being.

Secondary dimensions are more flexible. They include work background, education, income, marital status, military experience, religious beliefs, geographic location, and parental status. Primary dimensions of diversity are such a core part of us, and generally unchangeable, that any attack on one of those aspects is much more damaging to us than an attack on a secondary dimension. Secondary dimensions are usually more flexible. For example, we can change our education or our geographic location.

Criminals, as do other segments of the population, can and do use differences to offend, discriminate, and promote their particular agendas. Offenders use these differences to divide and conquer staff. When anyone treats people differently based on things they cannot change, it is particularly offensive. This results in hurt feelings and people becoming defensive. These things can polarize staff, compromising safety, security, and productivity.

The more broadly we define diversity, the more effectively we can use the definition to build a productive workforce. The current public scrutiny of diversity is due to changes in the American workforce, which started in the 1980s and continue today. The workforce is now made up of larger percentages of Hispanic, African-American, Asian-American, and other nonwhite populations or people of color. In addition, immigrants who come to the United States from all over the world, fleeing economic and political situations, are another aspect of the workforce. It also encompasses thinking styles, personality types, job function, professional specialties, and differences in life experience.

Historically, diversity education and training have provided new ways of looking at how to get work done and get along. One of the latest dimensions of diversity, identified as "generational," can bring an array of new perspectives into the workplace. When employees have open and honest discussion about their own generation, it can lead to a more harmonious and supportive communication climate among all generations. In the next decade, correctional organizations will have to recruit and develop retention strategies in new areas to insure the organization has the most competent staff and managers to keep it running smoothly. The best qualified in the next generation must be groomed to replace middle and upper management. An organization's survival and its ability to grow and flourish in the future largely will depend on teaching and training a new younger generation of managers on the in-and-outs of the organization.

Within the decade, a large number of baby boomers will be retiring. These will be captains, lieutenants, superintendents, chiefs, and other managers who take with them years and volumes of experience and skill. Members of the next generation, sometimes called "Generation X," are smaller in number, increasing the demand for those who have the maturity and desire and can be groomed and trained for these vacancies and needs.

Defining Diversity in a Broader Scope

Defining diversity in a broader scope expands the basic premise. Each person is a unique individual who brings a unique perspective and creative contribution to the task at hand. While ethnic and cultural differences are important, and collectively generate a significant number of complaints, if not the majority, they should not be focused on exclusively. However, diversity encompasses all differences between individuals.

"Cross generational" communications have a significant impact on the workplace. These communications show up in grievances, complaints, turnover, safety and security compromises, and other workplace maladies.

Each generation that comes to the workplace views its jobs differently: from their responsibilities; to how they give and receive information; and to how they plan their careers. The diversity in the generations represented in the workplace has a significant impact that is not just a passing fad but is here to stay. These generational differences can strengthen and empower individuals, organizations, and the community at large.

Diversity also has evolved from the affirmative side, influenced by what is articulated in law and policy (such as the Equal Employment Opportunity Commission guidelines, unlawful workplace harassment policies, sexual harassment policy, and so forth.). These laws and rules prohibit discrimination and help to level the playing field of opportunity and encourage inclusion in the workplace.

Affirmative action, valuing diversity, and managing diversity are separate points on the continuum of interventions designed to stimulate the inclusion of people from different backgrounds in an organization. The terms "affirmative action," "valuing diversity," and "managing diversity" are often confused, but it is important to differentiate among them.

Affirmative action is different from diversity because affirmative action is grounded in moral and social responsibility to amend the wrongs done in the past to those Americans who were not the majority population. These moral and social obligations are based on numerical measures and are designed to increase the representation of minorities and women in areas of employment where they previously were under-represented. (Disabled or handicapped issues are handled through the Americans with Disabilities Act.)

Valuing diversity builds on the critical foundation laid by workplace equity initiatives. The focus of this intervention is on recognizing the uniqueness in everyone, valuing the contribution that each can make, and creating an inclusive work environment where awareness of, and respect for, those of different cultures is promoted. It is the quality of the experience, rather than simply the participation rate of minority employees, women, or other groups within the workplace, that is paramount.

Managing diversity is different from both affirmative action and valuing diversity because it focuses on the business case for diversity. Under this scenario, capitalizing on diversity is a strategic approach to business that contributes to organizational goals such as profits and productivity. It does not involve any legal requirements and is not implemented simply to avoid lawsuits. Managing diversity moves beyond our valuing diversity in that it is a way in which we do business that aligns with other organizational strategic plans.

Affirmative action is based on an assimilationist model that focuses on getting people into an organization rather than changing organizational culture (valuing diversity). Subsequently, managing diversity, while based on cultural change, is a pragmatic business strategy that focuses on maximizing the productivity, creativity, and commitment of the workforce while meeting the needs of diverse consumer groups. While these three interventions build on one another, when affirmative action is tied together with valuing and/or managing diversity, diversity often becomes tainted by negative perceptions of affirmative action and therefore frequently is misunderstood. This leads to backlash, resistance, and polarization.

Valuing Differences

Valuing differences is the essence of synergy—combining the mental, emotional, and the psychological differences between people so they work together more harmoniously. And the key to valuing those differences is to realize that all people see the world, not as it is, but as they are. If I think that I see the world the way it is, why would I value differences? Why would I want to even bother with someone who is off track? My paradigm is that I am objective, I see the world as it is. Everyone else is buried by minutia, but I see the larger picture. That is why they call me a veteran, a supervisor, a manager, a professional, a teacher, I have "super-vision." Many people because of their title, position, education, and so forth fail or refuse to consider outside data or information. This outside data could enhance communication and provide a more efficient and effective way of doing a task or of handling responsibility.

Yet, if my paradigm is limited by my own conditioning, experiences, and influences, then, I am limited. Persons who are effective have the humility and ability to recognize their own limitations and to appreciate the rich resources available through the interaction with the hearts and minds of other human beings. These people value differences because they add to their knowledge and understanding of reality. When we are left to our own experiences, we constantly suffer from a shortage of data.

Is it logical that two people can disagree and both can be right? It is not logical; yet, it is psychological, and it is very real. Looking at a line drawing, you see the young lady; I see the old woman. We are both looking at the same picture, and both of us are right. We see the same black lines and the same white spaces. But we interpret them differently because of the ways that we have been conditioned to interpret them.

And unless we

- value the differences in our perceptions
- value each other
- give credence to the possibility that we are both right
- recognize that life is not always a dichotomous either/or
- realize that there are almost always third alternatives

we will never be able to transcend the limits of our conditioning. All I may see is the old woman. But I realize that you see something else. And I value you. I value your perception. I want to understand. So, when I become aware of the differences in our perceptions, I say, "Good! You see it differently! Help me see what you see."

The organization will not be helped if we have staff who only see the old woman. I do not want to communicate with someone who agrees with me; I want to communicate with you because you see something I do not see; you see it differently. I value that difference. This increases my own awareness; I also affirm you. This releases my negative energy that may have been invested in defending a particular position and enables me to act with synergy. Organizations and individuals within them must create an environment for synergy.

Valuing differences in a business or organization makes a strong case when it has to do with developing new products, markets, strategies, or techniques for developing staff, communicating, fostering safety, achieving goals, and fulfilling its mission. On an organizational level, smart managers value diversity to help them accomplish the task at hand. Bringing together staff with different viewpoints based on their cultural background, gender, ethnicity, and other diverse dimensions can allow for creativity that otherwise might not be put in motion. The greater the diversity of the organization, the greater is the potential for creative power. This is true if those differences can be channeled to achieve common goals, such as the efficient running of a facility or program. Valuing diversity can create new innovation and learning in organizations, which ultimately may result in a more humane and more stimulating work environment for all employees.

Valuing diversity through appreciation of differences can increase our resources and staff. Take for example the female officer who is not considered by her supervisor for a cell-extraction team or other custodial duties because of stereotypical thinking by the supervisor. Oftentimes, individuals in roles that are inconsistent with stereotypes suffer from others not being able to perceive them in other ways or positions. Some competent staff fail to get training and other opportunities because those that determine who is chosen cannot perceive minorities, women, or members of particular groups faring well in firearms training and other areas from which they have been historically excluded. Yet, such differences can contribute to safety, security, and productivity by introducing new styles of communication.

Managing Diversity

The differences each individual brings to the organization inevitably will cause conflict if they are not acknowledged. Conflict can be creative, if you can extract positive results from it. It also can generate more conflict, if not dealt with effectively.

First, only when we are comfortable with ourselves—our gender, race, position and so on, can we be comfortable with those who are different from us. This reflects the tenets of emotional intelligence and competence, which ultimately causes us to seek productive interaction. This entails not only self-awareness, self-regulation, and self-motivation in the interpersonal realm, but also perpetuates empathy, seeking to first understand then to be understood in the intrapersonal realm. This takes into account others' emotional disposition in their social interaction.

And second, for individuals to be successful, mutual respect for others must be the cornerstone of their operating philosophy. Quoting from and agreeing with Secretary Theodis Beck of the North Carolina Department of Correction, "We are in the people business."

Our definition of success is not based on a monetary bottom line or greed. It is the welfare of citizenry, offender, and staff. Respect and mutual respect is defined within the specific parameters; there is respect for our fellow human beings, respect for staff, supervisors, and offenders.

The author of *Seven Habits of Highly Effective People,* Stephen Covey, writes, "We are not our feelings. We are not our moods. We are not even our thoughts. The very fact that we can think about these things separates us from them and the animal world. Self-awareness enables us to stand apart and examine even the way we see ourselves. . . . It affects not only our attitudes and behaviors, but also how we see other people. It becomes our map of the basic nature of mankind."

Until we take how we see ourselves (and how we see others) into account, we will be unable to understand how others see and feel about themselves and their world. Unaware, we will project our intentions on their behavior and call ourselves objective. This significantly limits our personal potential and our ability to relate to others as well. But because of the unique human capacity of self-awareness, we can examine our paradigms to determine whether they are principle based or if they are a function of our conditioning.

Managing diversity means creating an atmosphere that internally and externally highlights the value of its diversity. To do this within an organization means striving to create an organization that:

- Accepts individual and group differences and works to value all differences
- Uses these differences to achieve goals
- Encourages communication
- Pulls everyone together, integrating each individual into the organization as a whole (Individual teams, groups, or departments should not be allowed to break away and isolate themselves from others.)
- Is characterized by mutual respect
- Allows each individual to speak for himself or herself

What Does Age Have to Do with It?

Those who study the differences among people of various ages use the following methods to distinguish them.

- The Veterans, born between the turn of the last century and the end of World War II (1900–1945), combine two generations that number about 75 million people.
- The Baby Boomers (1946–1964) are the largest population ever born in this country and number about 80 million.
- The Generation Xers (1965–1980) are a smaller but very influential population at 46 million.
- The Generation Yers (1981–1999) represent the next great demographic boom at 76 million.

While many generational experts have laid out age ranges to define the members of the generations, these should be considered just guidelines. There is no magic birth date that makes you a part of a particular generation. Generational personalities run much deeper. To understand the generations and what makes them the way they are, one needs to adopt "ageless thinking," and look at how each generation shares a common history. The events and conditions each of us experience during our formative years define who we are and how we view the world. As a result of our experiences, each generation has adopted its own "generational personality."

Certain conditions are the forces at work in the environment as each generation comes of age. The cold war, the Cuban missile crisis, the assassination of President John F. Kennedy—these were conditions that had an impact on the youth of many boomers, while Yers born after 1981 will remember "9/11," and the bombing of the World Trade Center. This generation will not remember the economic conditions that profoundly affected the wealth and health of citizens who lived through the Great Depression, or were raised by parents who did, and have permanently shaped their way of looking at the world.

Credit cards, long-term financing, and thirty-year mortgages were innovations that came after World War II and the Korean War. Earlier generations were far more conservative in their economic practices based on pre-war experiences, where money was tight and opportunities few.

Large-scale upheavals in the family, such as the rising divorce rate, or the number of single-parent families, and alternative families (same sex couples) all can play a role in shaping a generation's identity. Families of this type are more characteristic of the X and Y generation. Younger generations expect these differences; older generations have to learn to accept or reject them. These things have an impact on attitudes, behavior, and ultimately help to define each generation.

Generational Difference and Disturbance

Veterans grew up under the shadow of the Great Depression and felt lucky to have jobs. They bring values of patriotism, hard work, and respect for leaders to the workplace. Boomers have had to vie with 80 million peers every step of their career, which makes them competitive. They were raised by parents who taught them to believe they could make the world a better place so they tend to be idealists and come to the workplace with a strong desire to put their mark on things.

Generation Xers grew up seeing many businesses downsize or merge, and they learn that the last thing they could trust was the permanence of the workplace. By the time they got in the job market, the employer-employee contract was waning. (This was an agreement, at least implied historically in the workplace, where employers provided opportunity for advancement along with permanent and secure employment until retirement for those who were loyal and worked hard. In return, employees pledged allegiance for the duration or most of their employable years.)

Xers saw Social Security in jeopardy, and they often were told that they would not do as well as their parents had. As a result, they have to be recruited, rewarded, and managed differently from prior generations, if you hope to make them a contributing, loyal part of the workforce. Important to the management of the Xers is the type and frequency of feedback. Through two-way communication, through answering the "why" question, by being patient and tolerant enough to listen and then determine the value of what they have to say, the leader can harness the best from Generation Y.

You have to put the generations in an economic context. As a result of the long economic expansion of the 1990s creating a situation of almost full employment in the United States, many Generation Xers have been promoted rapidly and offered more financial and job growth opportunities than ever in history. In many instances, they have been able to demand that companies adapt to their way of doing things. This has created a cultural clash and resentment and backlash as the generations collided around issues of fairness and opportunity.

There is a talent war out there. Because Generation X is just a little over half the size of the Baby Boomers, regardless of what happens with the economy, fewer workers will be available in the age group poised to move into the management ranks. At the same time, a large number of Veterans and Boomers will be eligible to retire, leaving a leadership gap in the upper echelons of organizations with the Yers still a decade or two from being able to fill the management gap. The result is that businesses and other organizations will have to fight harder to recruit and retain the best and brightest employees. Organizations have to start to prepare for a mass exodus of know-how and experience that they are going to have to replace from a much smaller pool of talent that comes with a very different set of values and expectations.

Feedback: The Implications of Style and Culture

For the generations and other groups to work together in safe, productive, and harmonious environments, they need to communicate. To a degree and often uncharacteristic of some organizations, this communication needs to be two-way. Managers need to promote and use feedback and create feedback loops. The information we receive, the feedback, is the result of our behavior or communication, which allows us to adjust our future behavior and communications, forming a feedback loop. If we correctly perceive the relevant information being fed back to us, it will help us make accurate reads of others and adjust our communication or behavior accordingly.

Generation and culture, from sex and ethnicity to geography and education, largely influence the style and method of communication and feedback. The following are observations on how the generations differ in style and methods of communication and feedback.

Veterans are usually very cautious and tactful in the way they communicate to such a degree that Xers might not know what they mean. Veterans learned from the military model to button up and listen hard to the voice of authority. Obedience was paramount and talking back was out of the question. When we put these styles together, the feedback that a Veteran thinks is informative and helpful can seem formal and preachy to the Boomers and the Xers. Feedback that a Boomer thinks is fair and judicious can seem uptight and overly political to a Generation Xer or a Veteran. Feedback that a Generation Xer thinks is immediate and honest can seem hasty or even inappropriate to the other generations.

Clearly, the generations have not agreed on what the feedback contract is supposed to be. Organizations and managers often have not communicated or taken the time to recognize or acknowledge specific styles of feedback characteristic of a particular generation. Due to this lack of information or lack of bridging of differences, there is no accepted, implied, or written agreement on the type, style, or frequency of feedback. Veterans feel that no news is good news, Baby Boomers expect this feedback once a year with plenty of documentation (through performance appraisals). For the Xer, it is "Sorry to interrupt, but how am I doing?" and the Yers want feedback at their beck and call, by push button.

Choosing the Right Time and Place for Feedback

Veterans and Boomers have been coached on choosing the right time and place for feedback, to make others feel comfortable and receptive yet not so casual that the message is not taken seriously. Xers and Yers might suggest that the older generations "lighten up," although they could benefit from modeling this behavior in terms of time and place.

The younger generations (Xers and Yers) are used to getting and sending information via technology because they were born in a time of the Internet. They are used to having information sent and received so fast they often forget that the human hard drive does have a soft spot. They have not been taught some of the basics about time and place. Surveys show that a significant number of Xers never received training on giving and receiving feedback.

Additionally, many managers have not been trained in feedback; this applies not only to new managers but also to the older generations. All staff need to be trained in feedback—how to give it, how to receive it, and the appropriate behavior in feedback situations. Some people receive this training when they move up to management. However, this training on the rudiments of who the generations are and how to best communicate with one another would be beneficial to everyone. This type of training for managers and staff would improve communication and social interaction. It would help to eliminate older workers feeling that they are being challenged or threatened when a younger staff member asks the question "why?" or seeks an explanation or clarity. The older worker should be taught that the younger workers are not trying to be disrespectful. Through two-way communication, new and potentially more efficient and effective ideas can be entertained.

Older generations, accused of being stubborn and unwilling to change, often realize that situations and resources can dictate how feedback will be managed. This could result if there is an emergency or life-threatening incident. Also, some aspects of supervision and socialization whether with staff or offenders in the criminal justice system require trial and error. These may include such things as the individual responses to the environment, interaction with offenders and staff, and ethical decisions regarding undue familiarity or treatment.

Communication and Training Can Build Bridges and Improve Understanding and Cooperation

Studies referenced by Lancaster and Stillman (2002) have shown that top performers who receive regular feedback were more likely to stay on the job than those who did not. This shows that feedback plays a vital role in an employee's decision to stay in a job. These studies also show that lack of feedback was the number one cause of turnover among Xers. The need for more feedback is pressing at all levels. In a survey done by Lancaster and Stillman, generations were remarkably consistent about this. Over half of each generation said they do not get relevant feedback on the job. When generations of workers cannot talk to one another about performance and expectations, the organization suffers.

Without feedback, workers may not know how they are doing or where they are going. With feedback, managers and supervisors can communicate their goals or what they need in terms of performance. However, when feedback is lacking, frustrations turn to silences, which eventually, sadly, turn to severed relationships and often, severance altogether. Turnover rates increase the costs of doing business, which includes tangible expenses such as those of recruiting, hiring, and training new workers, as well as intangibles such as reduced morale and decreased efficiency. Providing information and training to employees on appropriate feedback presents real opportunity to significantly reduce the potential for problems between the generations.

When, Where, and How of Feedback

Feedback can be given in a number of ways: in person, by telephone, via e-mail or voice mail, in a written memo, or in a meeting. Managers cannot assume that employees innately know when, where, or how they should check in with their bosses. Feedback styles can be culturally determined, whether it is blatantly candid, tactfully careful, political, influenced by generational implications, or dictated by nationality or by organizational culture. It could prove very helpful for generations to talk about how feedback typically works in their culture or what are the expectations of feedback. Articulating and confirming your expectations up front is necessary so everyone knows what to expect.

By taking organizational culture and general culture into consideration, we can examine the lack of knowledge and information, by allowing for a dialog that emphasizes clear communication and articulated expectations. In assigning a task, have we asked questions to enhance or assure understanding? Do the individuals associated with the task have a familiarity with it? Members of certain cultures find it disrespectful to ask a question or talk back to a supervisor. So, if we are in a leadership role, we should take these things into account.

Information should flow in all directions in a learning organization. In criminal justice organizations, which are paramilitary organizations, the chain-of-command model does not necessarily advocate that feedback needs to travel up the ladder as well as down, which is something on which younger generations insist. Unlike Boomers and Veterans who would be reluctant to tell the boss what was wrong with the way the department was being managed, younger generations have less of a problem being up front with their higher ups. As Yers enter the workplace, the notion of questioning authority even while you respect it, will become more common due to this generation being asked their opinion while they were raised.

Information should flow in all directions, and no one should shoot the messenger when the feedback results in bad news. This will only happen if people of all generations feel clear on the expectations their managers have for them and safe in their execution.

Individuals have a tendency to migrate toward individuals and groups that are like them in terms of age, sex, or race. This familiarity enhances their comfort. Two co-managers, an Xer and a Boomer interviewed at the Cheridan Corporation, cited by Lancaster and Stillman, found that one way to create a safety net is to install individuals as "generation sounding boards." Research shows that younger people always take their problems to the Xer manager, while older employees tend to confide in the older manager.

Senior managers may employ methods to informally share information about the organization while at the same time letting employees share what is going on with them, in a nonthreatening setting. The most successful leaders find a way to let every generation be heard, even though it may mean being open to constructive criticism from someone considerably younger. At the same time, younger staff should work at making feedback to their older bosses and peers polite and respectful, nonthreatening, and nonconfrontational. And rather than be terribly impatient for an answer, give them time to reflect and prepare a response. Smart leaders will show that they listened and be willing to act on what they heard. Feedback from below is of no use if no one does anything about it.

Training

A significant number of both new managers and older managers have not been trained in providing feedback. Managers of all the generations need to be trained in feedback: how to give it; how to receive it; and the appropriate behavior in feedback situations.

Most people receive this training only when they move up to management. However, training on the rudiments of who the generations are and how we should communicate with one another would be beneficial to everyone.

The Power of Positive Feedback

Positive feedback is invaluable when trying to reach out to someone from another generation. All generations want and need positive feedback. No matter how hard it is to get tough messages out there, it is even harder to get positive messages out there. Veterans, even though they work because it is their job and seek no applause, still appreciate being told that their efforts were noticed and that they made a difference. Boomers are often busy giving feedback to dozens in other generations and their own, but they do not always receive any themselves, especially positive feedback.

Xers need positive feedback to let them know that they are on the right track. Some will admit that they have been promoted so fast that they are afraid to admit what they do not know.

Most likely, Yers have had lots of praise from managers who have talked to them about what they are doing right. This rewards good behavior and strengthens rapport. Positive and negative feedback needs to be given.

Cross-generational Mentoring and the Generational Interpreters

"Cross-generational mentoring" can offer new possibilities for both the younger and older worker. Younger members of the staff can learn from the experiences, skills, and feelings of an older mentor or friend and have someone they can trust and look up to for help and direction. Older workers (if they are willing to be open to change and objective) can find individuals in the younger generation who are not afraid to express their opinions and can serve as "generational interpreters."

The level of emotional intelligence and maturity of the "interpreter or representative" can enhance the creation of this type of dialog. These interpreters are able to assess and garner information from an intrapersonal perspective, which deals with self-awareness, self motivation, and self-regulation or control. The interpreters also operate from an interpersonal perspective and use empathy, which ultimately has an impact on social interaction. This includes good interpersonal communication skills, and seeking first to understand before being understood. This person would be the buffer, the mediator, the advocate, and the translator between the generations. This might include matters of language or terminology, dress, habits, and verbal and nonverbal behaviors. Identifying these individuals and creating dialog and collaboration could have an impact on policy and practices in the workplace. Employing cross generational interpreters could be a noteworthy consideration in a criminal justice organization where safety and security are so important, or in any organization that seeks a harmonious and productive work environment.

Where Do We Go From Here?

The author surveyed the thoughts, attitudes, observations, and concerns of correctional staff regarding generational behavior. The poll included officers, supervisors, managers, trainers, program staff, and custody staff. The responders were primarily Boomers along with some Veterans versus Xers with input from the Yers.

The survey responses paralleled the author's own observations and the types of observations cited and discussed in the literature. Members of the older generation repeatedly chided the lack of work ethic in younger workers, their wanting and even expecting instant gratification, their feeling of entitlement. They cited the younger workers' lack of ambition, wanting things their way, and their failing to look at the organization or their job as a team effort. One captain remarked the most annoying thing to him or the thing he would most like for them to understand is the impact of their actions and how they affect other staff. "I would like for them to understand that the need for unity and teamwork is a must for staff to survive under the difficulties that are placed on them daily in a prison setting."

Other observations about younger workers included their lack of cooperation, their being hard to motivate, and their cutting corners. "I don't see much loyalty to the job. They had no respect for authority and wanted to know what you could offer them."

With these types of observations, what did the older generation (Veterans and Boomers) like about the younger generation (Xers and Yers)? "One positive thing would be they are not afraid to express their opinions. I think my age group is more accepting of this quality than those who are older (Veterans). I believe that young people have good ideas and something to offer. My parent's generation is not as open to the idea that they could learn something from someone younger."

Another manager stated that their level of stress appears to fall way below the level of stress that Boomers seem to bear. This could be viewed as a good thing; however, he went on to say that their lack of worry could be interpreted as not caring about scheduling, a job, or anything else. Unfortunately, these traits could be deadly in the prison environment.

One correctional professional with a number of years in training and in the field stated, "Years ago, many correctional officers made a career of it, but few of our students now even stay a year. I don't want to stereotype, because we get some good young correctional officers, but the overall quality of our students has gone down."

When the sentiments of the younger generation (Xers and Yers) were tallied, the comments were that the older generations (Veterans and Boomers) were resistant to change and there was a tolerance of prejudice. When asked what they would like to change about the older group, one Xer responded, "I do not see the need to change anybody, it's an all around acceptance issue." Another commented that they have been around so long they do not seem to care and have forgotten the mission and goals of the organization. "They still need to be objective and open minded instead of just set in their ways. I do like that they have experience, but just because they have more experience, doesn't mean they know everything and they should be open to changes. Change is good."

Is the older generation so inflexible and set in their ways that they are not open to change, even if that change is good or necessary for survival and growth? Similarly, is the younger generation so naïve or arrogant that they are not amenable to the experience and lessons of time? Did their predecessors and their parents make them that way when they told them to stand up for their rights and for what they felt was right?

Clearly, there are cross-cultural communication problems. The generations have not signed off on a communication contract that stipulates two-way communication or understanding of feedback.

Maybe this task is one for the "Generational Interpreters," strategically placed in human resources, or who have a rotating shift assignment. They could be the counselors, communicative coaches, mentors, and models for other staff. Of course, there have to be representatives from the respective generations found in the workplace, who are fair, reasonable, and competent. Qualifications would require that they value differences. When they become aware of differences in perception, not only will they have the potential solutions rendered by the respective generations but also a potential third solution that comes from collaboration. And they should realize that when they solely look at the world through their eyes, they limit the data and the possibilities.

The vast majority of the inmate population ranges roughly from the ages of twenty-five to thirty-five. This greatly mirrors the staff being hired. They speak the same language, verbal and nonverbal. There are implications and connotations peculiar to this generation that can be of an enormous benefit. Older veteran staff bring volumes of experience and knowledge to an environment that can be compromised and potentially dangerous in many ways. Through collaboration, communication, and respect an atmosphere of safety and productivity can be achieved.

We as individuals, organizations, and communities must begin to assess our cultural intelligence and realize that we all have our own prejudices and bias. But there has to be a willingness and desire to recognize and to strive for a social, emotional, and cultural maturity. This maturity is manifested in how we treat one another in all our relationships regardless of the environment. The ability to distinguish between the records of bigotry and hate, that cause us to draw conclusions that dehumanize our fellow human no matter how they look, sound, originate, use the toilet, or simply because they are different in any respect, is a gift. To have the honesty and decency to admit when we do not know rather than make decisions based on ignorance or fear, we need to learn not only from our mistakes but also from the mistakes of others. We have to be open and willing to take risks to communicate with others who are different, and even with those who look like us, who were spun from our social loins but may see things differently.

We have to build and rebuild trust in our organizations and in our relationships; this is the premise and foundation of team building and teamwork. We have seen the level of trust diminished in our public organizations and bodies, in our businesses by the dishonesty and the toppling of our corporate giants. This permeates our relationships on a personal and professional level. There must be a contract of trust between individuals and organizations. Many need to be written and others rewritten, so that those who have a stake will have a clear and comfortable understanding and expectation of their behavior. Many would say that this is already articulated in law, policy, or ethical practice by reasonable people, but every now and again, we need to do a reevaluation and self-evaluation.

More Diversity than You Think

The definition of diversity expands beyond race, ethnicity, and sex, to include thinking style, educational background, geographic location, generations, avocation, lifestyle, sexual orientation, work experience, and more. Progressive organizations are working to expand their racial and ethnic diversity, while at the same time redefining diversity to include other factors and placing this emphasis in their recruiting. It is important to have a diverse team not just in race and gender but in skills and temperament.

Moving toward Diversified Wholeness

Whether approached from the direction of socio-political correctness, performance issues, an ethical imperative, or business strategy, the sought-for destination is a sense of wholeness. This wholeness is the understanding that is created when individuals and organizations experience a sense of oneness about who they are, what they are doing, how they are doing it, and where they are headed in the future.

Differences can create a certain kind of completeness, allowing all concerned to better understand who they are as individuals and as part of the organization. Diversity is influenced by competitive pressures, but it is ultimately the affirmation of the different talents we all bring to that larger game of life.

References

Covey, Stephen R. 1989. *The Seven Habits of Highly Effective People*. New York: Simon and Schuster.

Crouch, Bob. 2002. North Carolina Department of Corrections Staff Survey. Apex, North Carolina: Department of Corrections.

Holman, Larry. 1995. *Eleven Lessons in Leadership*. Lexington, Kentucky: Wyncom.

Lancaster, Lynne C. and David Stillman. 2002. *When Generations Collide*. New York: Harper Collins Publishers Inc.

Oakley, Ed and Doug Krug. 1991. *Enlightened Leadership*. New York: Simon and Schuster.

Chapter 4 Religious Diversity: A Kaleidoscope of Faiths

Reverend Doris Woodruff-Filbey,
Master of Divinity,
Director, Religious Services and
Community Involvement (retired)
Indiana Department of Correction
Indianapolis, Indiana

Remember the kaleidoscope you peered into as a child? An almost limitless variety of multicolored intricate designs would appear and evolve with only the slightest movement.

Like a kaleidoscope, religious expression in the United States is multifaceted and dynamic. The United States has been described as the most religiously pluralistic country in the world. The rise of immigration, the search for spirituality apart from organized religion, the shifting values of our society, and the freedom to develop and promote one's own unique faith contribute to this rich, and sometimes confusing, diversity. So, is it any wonder that our prisons are also experiencing this same phenomenon?

Historically, prisons had, at most, Catholic, Protestant, and Jewish chaplains who served only their own imprisoned "congregations." In today's prisons, correctional chaplains continue to offer services consistent with their own tradition, in addition to providing for the religious and spiritual needs of persons regardless of their religious affiliations, which may range from Adventists to Zoroastrians, Buddhists to Yoruba adherents.

The diversity within major religious movements adds to the complexity of this kaleidoscopic picture, and may require varying accommodations. For example, the Christian faith is divided into Roman Catholic, many liturgical and nonliturgical Protestant groups, Orthodox and Sabbatarian. Islam encompasses Sunni and Shiite (Orthodox), the

Nation of Islam, and the Moorish Science Temple of America, Inc. Jewish offenders may be Chasidic/Orthodox, Conservative, Reform, Reconstuctionists, or even Black Hebrew Israelites. Plains and Southwest traditions and the Native American Church represent Native American spirituality. Eastern religions include Buddhism, Hinduism, and Sikhism. Neopagan religions include Wicca and Asatru/Odinism. Newer expressions of spirituality include Spiritualism, Scientology, and Eckankar. And indigenous religions, in which culture interfaces with beliefs, include such faiths as Rastafarian, Santeria, and African-based religions such as Yoruba.

Why Provide for Such Diversity in Prison?

When training new staff on religious practices, they often ask why prisons accommodate so many different religions. Of course, the basic reason is that religious freedom, the right to believe and practice one's chosen faith, is protected by the First Amendment of the Constitution, even for inmates. Federal and state legislation may further define the religious rights of incarcerated persons.

The most current federal law regarding the practice of religion by inmates is the Religious Land Use and Institutionalized Persons Act of 2000 (S.2869), which states:

> No government shall impose a substantial burden on the religious exercise of a person residing in or confined to an institution . . . unless the government demonstrates that imposition of the burden on that person (1) is in furtherance of a compelling governmental interest; and (2) is the least restrictive means of furthering that compelling governmental interest.

This law applies in any case in which the substantial burden is imposed in a program or activity that receives federal financial assistance or affects commerce with foreign nations, among states, or with Indian tribes (which may relate to prison-industry programs).

In this legislation, religious exercise is defined as "any exercise of religion, whether or not compelled by, or central to, a system of religious belief."

Systems that are not subject to this federal legislation look to case law for guidance. In *O'Lone v. Shabazz*, 482 U.S. 342 (1987), the U.S. Supreme Court set such a standard. When a prison regulation impinges on inmates' constitutional rights, the regulation is valid if it is *reasonably related to a legitimate penological interest*. Because, in this case, the state of New Jersey had a legitimate interest in security, this interest outweighed the inmate's First Amendment claims.

State statutes also may require that offenders be allowed to practice their faith through such privileges as visitation from clergy/spiritual advisors, adherence to a religious diet, access to and possession of religious literature, the possession of items and symbols required for worship, and the right to observe holy days and holidays.

Prison systems also have policy and procedures that provide for the practice of religion, in an effort to ensure these constitutional and statutory rights are protected and provided for in an equitable manner. When the beliefs and practices are unfamiliar, and/or when there are few adherents of a faith group, the inmate may be denied the opportunity for religious expression, which could result in conflict, grievances, and unnecessary lawsuits. Procedures should provide for continuous review and authorization of new religious practices.

To ensure that diverse needs are met, the American Correctional Association's adult and juvenile standards for accreditation require that inmates/juveniles be provided the opportunity to participate in essential religious practices, limited only by concerns for safety and institutional order.

The American Correctional Chaplains Association, the oldest ACA affiliate (www.correctionalchaplains.org), is the professional organization for chaplains, volunteers, prison ministries, and religious-endorsing agencies. The American Correctional Chaplains Association supports and advocates for religious diversity in both inmate practice and chaplaincy. It also provides for certification of prison chaplains as an affirmation of their professionalism. Included in the certification process is attention to the chaplain's attitude toward and sensitivity to the accommodation of religious practices of faith groups other than his or her own.

Another reason to accommodate the diversity of religious practice is that it is believed that practicing a faith contributes both to the safety and security of a facility and to the rehabilitative process. Research in this area is limited, but studies do indicate a correlation between active participation in religious programs and reduced recidivism, fewer in-prison conduct reports, and a healthy adjustment to prison life.[1]

Incarceration, like other times of personal crises, may become a time of searching for spiritual fulfillment. Inmates who have had no religious background and those who no longer find helpful the religion of their childhood may seek a new spiritual path or look for enrichment by learning about and/or practicing more than one faith.

A negative aspect of this increasing diversity of religious practice is that there are those who seek a religion, often one that is little known or practiced, that reinforces their criminal thinking, behavior, and opportunity for promoting their agenda while incarcerated. This type of situation requires collaboration between chaplains and custody and/or security threat-group coordinators.

Respecting Differences

It is vital that the chaplain is willing to provide for the spiritual needs of all offenders with respect and integrity, as long as the religion is not injurious to self or others. Rev. David M. Schilder, in his book, *Inside the Fence*, writes:

> Since the chaplain carries out the role of pastor in a varied setting that is run in a military fashion by the secular government, it is incumbent upon her to have had some training in constitutional

law. She must have a clear legal understanding of just what the separation of church and state means. She must deeply and thoroughly understand that her position in the prison can in no way be used for the furtherance of her faith group's teachings over those of the other faith groups.

He continues:

Again, it needs to be said: if these religions are approached with the same respect that is shown the Christian denominations, the chaplain will again come away with her own faith enriched. She will come away understanding that there is more that binds us as brother and sister creatures of God than divides us."[2]

Chaplain Mohamed Afify, a chaplain at the State Correctional Institution at Waymart, Pennsylvania, a minimum-security prison, instituted a weekly multifaith forum headed by a panel of religious representatives from the community. The purpose of the program is to promote respect, tolerance, and understanding for and cooperation with the differing faith groups among inmates. During the wide-ranging dialog between inmates and panel members, their assumptions are challenged as inmates learn about each other's beliefs and practices. The Reverend William Gagas, a chaplain at Waymart for ten years, said the multifaith group has led to a "strong interest in religion" and "less anger and more tolerance among the inmates."

The purpose of the interfaith dialog is not conversion, but to provide a time to learn about one's own and others' religion. One inmate reports that the program has helped him and others turn their incarceration into a positive situation. Afify also reports that inmates are more friendly and receptive to him. Even one of the panel members considered her participation an "eye-opening experience."[3]

Current events also may provide an opportunity, or even a need, for interfaith dialog. The attack on the World Trade Center towers and the Pentagon on September 11, 2001, led one Indiana chaplain to change the nature of his bible study that day to an interfaith dialog and prayer service which helped defuse strong feelings between the inmates regarding their religious affiliations and differences.

Chaplains may also have to deal with staff attitudes toward inmate religious practice if there is evidence of intolerance, ridicule, or proselytizing. Efforts, including staff training, to promote tolerance and respect for religious diversity, may be required.

Managing Religious Diversity

Allowing for and managing this growing diversity of religious practice may have legal, operational, and programmatic impact in the correctional system. Deciding how to and which religious practices to authorize or restrict may involve a number of considerations.

A mission statement for the religious services division of a prison system may help provide guidance in the decision-making process regarding diversity of practice and related programs. For example, the mission statement of the Oregon Department of Corrections Religious Services states:

> The mission of the Religious Services Division is to provide a spiritual environment within the Oregon DOC that will model, promote, and encourage individuals to develop spiritually toward a redemptive and rehabilitative end.

To avoid unnecessary lawsuits, prison systems must have in place procedures that reflect the legal requirements regarding requests related to religious practices. This is increasingly important as the diversity of practice increases. These issues should be addressed when considering the restriction of a religious practice:

- Is this an exercise of religion?
- Is there a substantial burden on the inmate's free exercise of religion?

- If both are met, is there a compelling government interest furthered by the burden?
- Is the government interest met in the least restrictive way?

Additional information about applicable case law related to these issues is included in the National Institute of Corrections' training program, "Training Today's Correctional Leaders to Meet Tomorrow's Challenges."[4]

A method to track the religious preferences of offenders and their participation in programs both by facility and systemwide is needed to assist in the equitable provision of resources. Methods of evaluating or auditing religious programs and allowed practices at the facility level may need to be developed to ensure that the chaplaincy program is responding to the diversity of spiritual needs of the population.

Adding to the complexity of accommodating spiritual practices is the fact that some religions, such as Buddhism, encourage persons to hold to their faith tradition while engaging in spiritual practices of another faith. Native Americans who follow their spiritual path may also adopt and practice a Christian faith. These blended practices may require a procedure for accommodation.

Programs often compete for time, space and supervision. Making room in the schedule for a growing diversity of religious services may compound this problem. To serve all faith groups, some states have limited religious programs to one worship and one study per week. However, this may not sufficiently serve the faith group with the largest population. An equitable, or reasonable, solution that accommodates the assessed needs of each group should be the goal.

Finding community resources for leadership of these diverse faith groups, or allowing inmate leadership, is a concern. Prisons may be located in rural communities that lack the diversity of religious practice represented in the prison population. If inmates are allowed to lead services of worship or study, procedures that clearly state eligibility requirements, length of service, and limits of authority must be promulgated. Careful monitoring of inmate-led services may be essential to prevent misuse by those whose agendas are other than spiritual.

The operational impact of growing diversity of religious practices requires collaboration between chaplaincy and custody staff. There may be legitimate security concerns related to the accommodation of some religious practices. For example, the Native American sweat lodge ceremony requires inmates to be out of sight of security while in the lodge. A fire pit, heated rocks, and tools for handling them are necessary. Yet, this ceremony has been accommodated in many prisons with few or no conduct-related problems because inmates consider it a sacred ceremony and take responsibility for protecting that sacredness. Some faith groups may consider sacramental wine or tobacco (which may be contraband in smoke-free facilities) a required practice. A process for evaluating both the operational and programmatic aspects of accommodating each newly requested ceremony must be in place.

Growing diversity requires the careful evaluation of accommodating the practices of faith groups that are not common in community, or which may practice covertly, to prevent the promotion of racist beliefs or the masking of security threat group activity. Any restrictions and/or accommodations should be carefully researched and documented according to applicable legislation. Faith practices may include religious diets, fasting requirements, ceremonial/religious items and symbols for both personal and congregate worship and identification, means of celebrating holy days and holidays, and work restrictions. All this requires sound management practices and the need for collaboration among chaplaincy and operational staff.

This growing diversity may require prison systems to diversify their chaplaincy corps, or contracts may be established to provide for the spiritual needs of particular faith groups under the direction of an administrative/institutional chaplain.

Some state departments of correction and the Federal Bureau of Prisons have developed handbooks of religious beliefs and practices to inform offenders and staff about the differing faith groups. Included may be minimum requirements for practice and possession of religious property while incarcerated. This allows for consistency of practice throughout a system, and helps prevent lawsuits related to religious practice. The State of Washington Department of Corrections has long provided such a handbook, which has served as a model for other states. The Federal Bureau of Prisons recently completed an extensive handbook, available to other prisons from the National Institute of Corrections.

Another movement is the establishment of faith-based housing units. Initially these units have primarily been addressed toward one faith. However, this concept provides an opportunity to house offenders of differing faiths together as they learn to apply and live by their doctrines of faith in a holistic way in preparation for a successful transition to the community. This multifaith model used by the Marion Correctional Institution in Marion, Ohio, and the Federal Bureau of Prisons promotes greater tolerance and respect for differences, both cultural and religious.

Volunteer management also may be affected by this growing religious diversity. There will be a need to recruit volunteers to help serve these faith groups, and to accommodate and promote understanding of any distinguishing religious attire and cultural practices. For example, Muslim women are required to wear the hijab, a scarf that covers the head, neck, and shoulders. The scarf can be removed only in the presence of other women.

Native Americans may wear or bring into the facility items that are considered desecrated by being touched by others. Search procedures for volunteers should reflect respect for these types of religious and/or cultural practices.

Volunteer training also may need to include information about the diversity of religious beliefs and practices of the inmate population to help volunteers understand the need to accommodate diverse practices, promote respect for differences, and avoid proselytizing.

Some correctional systems, such as the Texas Department of Criminal Justice, have developed a religious practices committee consisting of central office administrative staff from operations, chaplaincy, legal, and food service, to evaluate and authorize practices. The Washington Department of Corrections has developed a religious advisory council made up of community representatives of the various faith groups to advise regarding legitimate practices, accommodations for practice, and to provide other related support and advisory services.

Conclusion

Sadly, within the kaleidoscope of religions there are those who mix politics and religion in an effort to impose their beliefs on others. Intolerance has led to many "holy" wars. Presently this intolerance, and the hatred it elicits, threatens our world.

This phenomenon can be avoided in the prison setting with effective management, equitable treatment among faith groups, and respect for differing beliefs and practices. Even better, bridges of care and service can be built between religious communities inside prison walls and with those on the outside in a joint effort to provide for prison safety and security and successful community reintegration.

To accomplish this, the following will be required:

- A correctional system that continues to respond to this diversity from both an operational and a programmatic perspective
- Effective management and oversight of the system's religious services program
- Creative program development designed for the incarcerated population that addresses the principles of risk, need, and responsivity—criminogenic needs and strengths (for example, antisocial history, antisocial companions, antisocial attitudes, and antisocial personality)
- A professional correctional chaplaincy staff that respects, supports, and advocates for diversity and is sensitive to operational concerns

- The support of and cooperation with nonprison faith communities, local leaders, and authorities
- Religious endorsing bodies that understand the requirements of prison chaplaincy and will consistently affirm these when considering candidates for endorsement

What is before those who work with this growing religious diversity is both a challenge and an opportunity, constantly changing and evolving.

Endnotes

[1] Clear, Todd R., Bruce D. Stout, Harry R. Dammer, Linda Kelly, Patricia L. Hardyman, and Carol Shapiro. 1992. Does Involvement in Religion Help Prisoners Adjust to Prison? *NCCD Focus*. November.

[2] Rev. David M. Schilder. 1999. *Inside the Fence: A Handbook for Those in Prison Ministry*, New York: Alba House, pp. 52 and 56.

[3] Carla Kucinski. Multifaith Classes Teach Prisoners to Respect Differences. *Press and Sun-Bulletin*, Binghamton, New York.

[4] Training Today's Correctional Leaders to Meet Tomorrow's Challenges (01-P3801), Correctional Religious Programs, U.S. Department of Justice, National Institute of Corrections.

References

McDaniel, Jay B. 1996. *With Roots and Wings: Christianity in an Age of Ecology and Dialog*. Maryknoll, New York: Orbis Books.

Ontario Multifaith Council on Spiritual and Religious Care. 2000. *Multifaith Information Manual, 4th Edition*. Available at www.library.omc.on.ca.

O'Connor, Thomas P. and Nathaniel J. Pallone, eds. 2003. *Religion, the Community, and the Rehabilitation of Criminal Offenders*. Binghamton, New York: Haworth Press.

Thangaraj, M. Thomas. 1997. *Relating to People of Other Religions: What Every Christian Needs to Know*. Nashville: Abingdon Press.

Wilson, Andrew, ed. 1991. *World Scripture: A Comparative Anthology of Sacred Texts*. A Project of the International Religious Foundation. St. Paul, Minnesota: Paragon House.

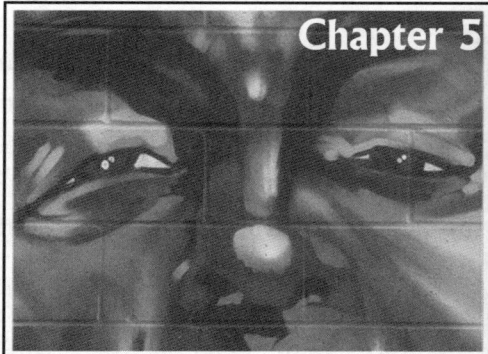

Chapter 5 | Latinos in Corrections: One View

Ana T. Aguirre
Senior Trainer
Texas Juvenile
Probation Commission
Austin, Texas

"Listen, being a Mexican-American is tough. Anglos jump all over you if you don't speak English perfectly; Mexicans jump all over you if you don't speak Spanish perfectly. We gotta be twice as perfect as anybody else! . . . I'm serious. Our family has been here for centuries and yet they treat us like we just swam across the Rio Grande! I mean we gotta know about John Wayne and Pedro Infante. We've gotta know about Frank Sinatra and Augustine Lara. We gotta know about Opera and Christina. Anglo food is too bland, and yet when we go to Mexico we get the runs, now that to me is embarrassing! . . . Japanese-American, Italian-American, German-American, their home town is on the other side of the ocean. Ours is right next door, right over there, and we got to prove to the Mexicans how Mexican we are, and we gotta prove to the Americans how American we are. We gotta be more Mexican then the Mexicans. We gotta be more American than the Americans both at the same time! It's exhausting, man! Nobody knows how tough it is to be Mexican-American!"

When Edward James Olmos, who was playing the role of Abraham Quintanilla, Selena Quintanilla-Perez' father in the movie *Selena*, made the above-quoted statements, those of us who have lived this experience could relate. And, we laughed because it is true, regardless of where you work.

In responding to the request by the American Correctional Association to write a short chapter regarding the topic "Latinos in

Corrections," this author realized, in conducting her search for written literature or research, that there was nothing out there. She contacted various colleagues, and they acknowledged the literature was not there. Therefore, what little there is to offer in this brief article is based on her personal experience and those she has the privilege of knowing and briefly interviewing.

Much of her experience is based from the perspective of a first-generation Mexican-American female. And, like many fellow Americans, her "Mexican" heritage is a combination of Spanish, French, Aztec, and Mayan blood lineage. Like many, as she has matured and for the sake of ensuring her children remember their heritage, she has made a point to acknowledge her complete heritage.

The views noted here do not necessarily reflect the views of other "Latinos/Latinas," or "Hispanos/Hispanas," whatever category we have placed ourselves in or been placed in by those coexisting within our respective communities. For the purposes of this reading, this author is referring to this ethnic group as *Latinos*. The reader needs to recognize the critical importance of the various differences that may exist among the Latino ethnic groups. Latinos could include, but are not limited to, those with origins in Mexico, Cuba, Puerto Rico, Ecuador, Honduras, Nicaragua, and El Salvador, regardless of how many generations have lived in the United States. The implied common bond is language, whether we are fluent in it or not, although the dialects vary from region to region or country to country. From here, our differences become even more pronounced depending on our skin tone/color, texture or color of our hair, eye color, or other physical features.

As a Latina who has worked in corrections for nearly twenty years, there have been moments of laughter to ones of extreme sadness. Even today, when this author realizes and appreciates how much we have accomplished, something happens that reminds us that there is still more work to be done. As recently as this year during an interagency meeting, an agency representative stated that they needed to work harder at hiring "Hispanic" speaking staff! The author was not present,

66

but what is even harder to understand is that there were others there that either did not recognize the error or chose not to speak out. It is times like this that we need to step up to the plate and address the need for cultural diversity education and sensitivity, and, if necessary, seek clarification.

In speaking with several colleagues in the system, one of the best things about being Latino and in this job is the opportunity to model for others. There is a way for us to open doors and help one another in this field. As Latinos, we can shape policy and influence the way we provide services in the community. We are more sensitive to our (Latino) issues, and as public servants, we can bring up issues that others do not know how or want to talk about.

On the other hand, the challenges include growing up in the process, which often makes for long days, at the same time balancing our obligations to our families. As one colleague stated, "Take care of your real priorities in life."

Does It Matter?

Schools are not the only ones responsible for educating members of our society. The obligation of educating members of our society belongs to all of us. While working as a juvenile probation officer, many of the kids got themselves suspended and/or expelled just to get out of school and the author realized that supervising "her children" while they were not in school made it harder for everyone (law enforcement, parents, and herself). On her own initiative, and with her chief's approval, she secured some educational materials and told her children that on those days they were not in school, as a result of a suspension or expulsion, they were to come to her office for tutorials. They soon learned that regular schoolwork was better than a juvenile probation officer's version of academia. History was a great topic, particularly when they were learning things they were not being taught at their grade level.

One day, three of her children, who happened to be Mexican-American, showed up at her office during school hours. When she asked them why they were not in school, they informed her that they had gotten into a disagreement with the teacher during class. She let them know that they were not supposed to argue with the teacher. One of the young men then told her that the material the teacher was using was incorrect and all they were trying to do was tell her. Another jumped in and stated, "Miss, we know she's wrong because of what you taught us!" The author was speechless.

The class was discussing the history of the Alamo and the teacher was showing a video that did not reflect the fact that Mexicans were also helping defend it. When her three kids asked her where the Mexicans were in the video, she told the class that there were no Mexicans defending the Alamo. My three young men tried to tell her she was wrong. The teacher got angry and sent them to the office. As a result, they were suspended. Needless to say, the author had to contact the principal and let him know about her tutorials and that her children were right. She asked that they be allowed to return to the classroom without any consequences. She knew that day that her three children were proud, but not more than she was of them.

As an auditor for the American Correctional Association (ACA), the author commends the contributing authors of the ACA's Standards for their sensitivity to the various cultural differences of those who are recipients of correctional ser-vices. Recognizing the language barriers, there are provisions for the development of multilanguage information and the provision of bilingual speakers to ensure that individuals are fully informed of their rights, services available, and how the juvenile/criminal justice process works.

Working with Latino Offenders and Victims

As we work with individuals who come from backgrounds dissim-ilar to us, we may come to the realization that people will have different reactions to us based on their personal experiences. For example, Latinos that come from countries in which they have been oppressed by the justice system could expect the same treatment in this country. Such might be the case of a parent who was from a country such as that who had his child detained for allegedly committing an offense. The probation officer seeing the fear in his face would need to assure the parent that his child would be fine and there would be no harm to him. This father who was genuinely fearful for his son stated he would contact the League of United Latin Americans (LULAC), a civil rights organization for Hispanics, and seek help. The officer let him know that that would be fine and to come to the office the next morning. When the father showed up at the office the next morning, he thought he recognized her and asked the officer if she was the president of the local LULAC Chapter. The officer said "yes." The family now knew they could focus on the offense and not worry that their son would be harmed.

Unfortunately, that is not the case in all circumstances. A recent article in *Parade* magazine discussed the Senate Judiciary Committee hearing on the treatment of children who fall under the care of the U.S. Immigration and Naturalization Service (INS). The Immigration and Naturalization Service placed more than 4,600 foreign minors in detention last year. The largest group was Latin Americans caught crossing the Mexican border. More than 30 percent of these children are incarcerated among violent criminals. Many are deported without their claims for asylum ever being heard even if they fled life-threatening abuse in their homelands. Congress sought to address the treatment of children in the custody of the Immigration and Naturalization Service because based on the testimony presented before Congress, these children whose primary language is not English, had been subjected to abuse.

For those of us who work in corrections, being bilingual can be a blessing or a curse, depending on how you see it. It is a curse in situations where you are required to maintain the same workload as your fellow monolingual colleagues and/or if you are not compensated or appreciated for this skill. Being bilingual is a blessing when you know you are part of the answer in providing quality service delivery, whether it is informing the offenders and their families of their rights, or describing the program and the rules.

One area given high publicity is the number of crimes committed by minorities. What should be equally, if not more importantly recognized, is the fact that the victims of these same offenders are also minorities. As staff members in the corrections arena, what better way to provide a balance in our work than by helping victims through translation services at crime scenes, in courtrooms, in counseling offices, at the funeral home, battered women's shelters, day labor camps, victim/offender mediations, and in other programs that offer victims' assistance? Many times, these crimes go unreported because the victims do not know the system or fear it. For example, the police department in Austin, Texas, developed a process which would allow undocumented residents to report a crime without the threat of deportation lingering over their heads. This was in response to a number of murdered victims who were singled out because they had to carry large amounts of money on their persons since they could not readily set up bank accounts.

Of course, the greatest benefit of being bi/multilingual is staff safety. This is not only an issue for the individual staff members, but more so for management. In situations where the population being served uses another language, for safety and security alone, it is in the organization's best interest to properly staff these programs with individuals who can speak in their native language to those who are incarcerated. This is applicable, whether the staff work in a secure facility or are supervising offenders within their communities.

On the other hand, as in other cultures, there are those occasions in which the families of Latino offenders and the offenders themselves, when faced with a Latino who works in corrections, will make the wrong assumption that we will be more loyal to them because of our similar culture rather than to the Constitution of the United States. That is an area quickly corrected when we remind them of the accountability process and can tell the victims of their the rights in Spanish.

Latinas in Corrections

A colleague once told me that he knew Latina women had it hard in that they were stepping outside traditional roles of staying at home and being submissive. Working in corrections requires us to be willing to take chances and break barriers, to stand up and speak out for our own individual beliefs. Not only do we have to justify our nontraditional roles to our families, our male colleagues, including Latino males, but imagine the surprise when we encounter some of the Latino offenders and their families. We know we are viewed differently when it is known that our jobs require a formal piece of identification such as a badge. It can really get "interesting" if they know we also carry a gun. For any female in this field, this can be a delicate situation.

It takes a little getting used to being told that we need to go back to the kitchen. On the other hand, there are those "poetic justice" moments like the one a Latina juvenile probation officer recalled. Her two juvenile probationers (brothers) came in with their father. When she inquired where their mother was since this was to be a family session, the father sarcastically stated, "She's home where she belongs. I had to beat her last night for not cleaning the house." The boys snickered. The officer then looked directly at the boy's father and stated, "It's a good thing you're not my husband, you'd be in jail right now!" The boys looked to their father in shock. He said nothing, obviously also shocked that a woman had said this. Then, he became embarrassed since this happened in front of his sons and there was nothing he could do. This family required more intervention, but eventually those two boys learned more than just the legal consequences of their offense.

What is critical in these types of situations is the message that we relay to those who are not necessarily familiar with the American legal system. It is not an issue of, "your people are just like that," because we all know domestic violence exists in all cultures and economic levels.

The emphasis of the message is that any victim, female or male, can report domestic violence and the perpetrator will face consequences. Domestic violence perpetrators may be of any race or nationality. The correctional worker has a responsibility to let perpetrators know that what they are doing is illegal and can get them jailed. Additionally, although immediate family members or friends may not be close by, the victims should have access to varied resources not only for themselves but also for their children.

Cultures Clashing

As we develop within the corrections discipline, it is important that we recognize and remember where we have been and what we are working towards. In the 1960s, the "melting pot" theory was abundant. People were led to believe that the assimilation of cultures was the best for all. Today, there is an emphasis on pluralism and recognizing the uniqueness of these cultures. What we are finding ourselves dealing with is more of an amalgamation—a stew not a meltdown. After all, how many of our clients come in with parents of two different races or ethnicities? Then we find ourselves trying to determine what box they fit into for data purposes. Some correctional staff find themselves in that dilemma.

Our first responsibility is to ourselves. The author recalls having her name "Anglicized" in the way it was pronounced throughout her school career. No matter how hard she tried, she could not make the teachers, fellow students, or their parents pronounce her name the way her parents intended it. Her personal goal was finally accomplished when she went to college and insisted that her name be pronounced correctly. Even today, this is an ongoing struggle. What has been wonderful about this experience is that for the most part, most individuals honor this request and sincerely make an effort to make the correct enunciation. Most importantly, clients of our systems see this and she gets a sense of pride when they acknowledge that she is proud of her ancestry.

Then, there are those that are called upon to represent our ethnicity, whether through a hiring process, board member selection, committee membership, or task force assignments. Yes, we are quotas. There are those who consider this offensive. Then there are those that insist that only when all groups are equally represented do we stand a better chance of being fairly represented. This author has been around long enough to acknowledge that it was these quota requirements that presented opportunities to her that would otherwise have prevented her from even being considered.

Another critical point is the importance of exposing everyone to the various Latino cultures. It is also through the cross-representation of the various Latino cultures that we can also learn about special cultural/religious events and holidays. For example, Cinco de Mayo is a Mexican holiday; Cesar Chavez spoke for the poor farm laborers and many others; Che Guevara is a hero to many. What we need to do is take the time to talk about the impact these individuals and many more that have had an impact on our history and our future.

Where do we go from here? What obligations do we have to ourselves as professionals while at the same time we hold on to that part of our lives that make us who we are? The following suggestions may help.

- Increase your visibility as a community leader—be proactive. You need to be seen as more than as a "corrections officer." For many more we are seen as role models.
- Organize! Currently, discussions are taking place to create a national organization that would speak to Latino issues. The American Correctional Association, hopefully, will facilitate this endeavor.
- Latinas need to raise issues specific to Latina corrections officers and also include issues pertaining to Latina offenders.

- Address issues recently noted through the news media regarding medical issues for Hispanics. These issues will have an impact on the types of services we will need to be prepared to address in the future.
- Give equal attention to victims' issues in the Latino communities.

References

Relin, David Oliver. 2002. Who Will Stand Up For Them? *Parade Magazine*, 5-6, August 4.

Robert Catc and Moctesuma Esparxa (Producers), Peter Lopez (Co-Producer) and Gregory Nava (Writer/Director). 1997. *Selena* [Motion picture]. United States: Warner Brothers.

Chapter 6 Latinos in Corrections: Another View

Raul S. Banasco
Warden
Florida State
Department of Corrections
Orlando, Florida

First let me start by stating that I am very proud of being a "CUBAN-PUERTO RICAN-AMERICAN."

I was born and raised in the Bronx, New York. My parents are of Cuban and Puerto Rican descent. In 1987, at the age of twenty one, I moved to Orlando, Florida. I am honored to contribute to this chapter, "Latinos in Corrections."

In 1988, when I started my career in the law enforcement field of corrections, I was determined to make this life-altering choice for my benefit and for those of Latin descent. There were very few Latinos in corrections at that time in the Central Florida area, and for the few that were in corrections, the majority held line staff/entry level positions within their agencies. Latinos in corrections have walked and continue to walk the longer road of career paths. We, as Latinos, have to prove that our English communication skills, knowledge of the positions we hold, dedication, loyalty, and commitment are far more accurate than those of any other race.

I can remember going through the Correctional Officer Academy in 1988. As I started my Academy class, I remember one of the challenges that faced me just because I was Latino. I was approached by a Caucasian officer going through the same academy class. He said to me, "El Chico, do you know how to speak and read English?" My reply to him was that I was fully aware of the job expectations and requirements. His reply back was that I didn't speak like a Mexican. He then asked, "What are you?" I paused for a moment as I looked at him and stated, "What ignorance!" I was twenty-two years old at that time, and I have never endured such harassment nor was I ever asked such a question of ignorance and arrogance.

Over the years, I have come to observe society as a whole. Some who are not educated or knowledgeable do not know that Latinos are not just of one race. Latinos come from a wide stretch of locations such as Cuba, Puerto Rico, Mexico, Spain, the Dominican Republic, and various other places.

If someone were to do research on "Latinos in Corrections," what would they discover? One perhaps would conclude that there is a lack of Latinos in corrections.

As I have continued my career in corrections, I have come to realize that the Anglo and African-American races were united to a certain degree when it came to addressing issues, concerns, and career advancements within corrections. However, Latinos fail to be a united force when addressing the same concerns.

As I have become knowledgeable in the corrections field and have spoken to my fellow Latino colleagues, I have always encouraged them to be more forthright, to seek a higher education, and to strive for possible career advancements. What has frustrated me most over the years, for the Latinos, is the lack of responsiveness from those who hold professional positions. It is almost as if Latinos need to possess an additional set of skills to effectively perform their jobs. Even though we are bilingual, and some are multilingual, there is still a problem with communication across cultures.

There should be more diverse training towards multi-cultures within the correction field. Having been brought up living under two different cultures, I can see that the diverse, but yet so common ground between Cuban and Puerto Rican lifestyles is remarkable. The Cubans are known as the "hard working" type. They are family oriented, accept no handouts, and establish a firm foundation at home and in the workplace. They are determined to complete their education for self-betterment and productive professionalism. The Cubans are stereotyped for their cuisine of black beans and white rice, along with the Cuban sandwich. There is a struggle in political practices among the Cubans since the governing organization of Fidel Castro took over in Cuba.

Puerto Rico, however, has for a long time been a commonwealth of the United States. For the most part, the Puerto Ricans come from a "lower economic lifestyle." They believe in family unity. They are willing to swallow pride for acceptance. A large number of Puerto Ricans are not as strong on education for advancement. Their main cuisine consists of yellow rice and beans.

The Latino race has insignificant representation in the management field of corrections in the State of Florida. Unless you are very fortunate, "the perfect job is not going to just drop in your lap." We as Latinos have to get out there and find it, and work hard for it. There are concerns that Latinos are not educated enough to attain a professional high-paying job. Yet, I always thought that the American dream was inclusive of the Latino community.

To remedy this stereotype, we must seek solutions to the problems of race and class. We must continue to stand up for what is right so that things will be better for those Latinos who are coming up after us. We need to provide the Latino with great exposure and access to successful professionals like ourselves. If we do nothing but sit on the sidelines and watch time go by in our own career fields, the next generation of Latinos may not be so fortunate. We need to recognize that we have not achieved our accomplishments merely due to our talents, individual efforts, and sacrifice, but rather due to the collective efforts of others in openings doors of opportunities for the Latinos in corrections. We need to start mentoring to contribute to the continued development of driven Latinos.

If you are Latino, ask yourself this question: What have we done, as Latinos, in the last year, the last six months, last week, or even yesterday, to ensure that the next Latino considering a career in corrections, and who is just like we were years ago, will be sitting where we are today. We need to stand up for our convictions and help those who are embarking on our corrections field of the future.

National Organization of Hispanics in Criminal Justice

After participating in several American Correctional Association accreditation audits, and serving on several national criminal justice boards, a few fellow colleagues and I observed the lack of Latinos in the management levels of both law enforcement and in the corrections field. Therefore, due to the lack of Latinos in corrections, we formed the National Organization of Hispanics in Criminal Justice. It was chartered by a core group of Hispanics in 2003 as a nonprofit corporation dedicated to promoting high professional standards for criminal justice agencies and criminal justice personnel. The keystone of the National Organization of Hispanics in Criminal Justice is to foster an interchange of information and training between professionals in law enforcement, the courts, corrections, probation and parole, juvenile justice, and interested citizens.

This year the National Organization of Hispanics in Criminal Justice's main objective is to focus the attention of its members and the citizens on the needs of the criminal justice system. The emphasis at the federal, state, and local level has been on the variety of challenges facing the criminal justice system.

The National Organization of Hispanics in Criminal Justice is directed by an executive board which includes a president, vice president, treasurer, and a secretary. Administrative and membership functions are provided by the executive board and a membership chairperson. The organization continues to expand its membership nationally.

Our specific objective is to provide a mechanism for a meaningful interchange of information among the disciplines of the criminal justice system nationally for Hispanics and other minorities. The National

Organization of Hispanics in Criminal Justice will keep citizenry informed and educated as to the purposes, goals, achievements, and challenges of the criminal justice system. The organization will solicit volunteer involvement and perform and promote community service. It will promote high standards of professional practice in the criminal justice system and conduct na-tional seminars, workshops, and institutes, and other training programs for criminal justice practitioners

The mission of the National Organization of Hispanics in Criminal Justice is to strive to promote equality for people of Hispanic decent and other minorities in the criminal justice field through examination of members' needs, concerns, talents, and strengths.

The National Organization of Hispanics in Criminal Justice publishes a newsletter, *La Voz* (*The Voice*) quarterly. Individual members are kept informed about activities, legislative action, and current events that may be of interest to criminal justice practitioners by an informational newsletter.

Membership is open to all criminal justice personnel and all interested citizens who support the goals and objectives of the National Organization of Hispanics in Criminal Justice. If you are interested in becoming a member, please contact a representative of the organization at 518-561-3245.

Chapter 7 American Indians

Gayl R. Edmunds
Program Director
Indian Alcoholism
Treatment Service
Wichita, Kansas

The staffing patterns of any institution should reflect proportionately the populations that they serve. Thus, the state and federal prison systems should make all attempts to adhere to a policy of hiring personnel that meet this standard and match the various inmate ethnicities in America's corrections system.

Personnel working at any institution bring their own set of values, beliefs, spirituality, and cultural mores to the job. People often misunderstand or take for granted that not everyone shares similar values, beliefs, spirituality, and cultural mores. This mistaken belief can create resentments and sometimes clashes that can lead to a hostile working environment.

Within this context, this chapter is aimed at assisting corrections officers to better understand American Indian personnel working within the system. There is no current compilation of the numbers of correctional staff with an American-Indian heritage.

Practically all institutions have standards and practices for the handling of American Indian sacred items. However, there are no standardized or universally accepted policies and procedures for the handling of sacred items. The U.S. Bureau of Prisons' *Report of the Chaplaincy Work Group* (1992) stated, "The Work Group concluded that the most important issues facing American Indian inmates could best be addressed through further training and education of Bureau of Prisons' employees."

American Indians have experienced a complete and total cultural upheaval. Beginning in 1492 to date, there remains a lack of understanding of the American Indian. The dominant culture has portrayed the American Indian in two contexts. One is of the "noble savage," as often portrayed in books and Hollywood movies. The other is as a bumbling caricature epitomized as a "drunk" and, at this writing, portrayed as sports mascots. This view is further fostered by an education system that rarely includes the American Indian's side of the story.

Following the capitulation of the various tribes and the ending of "The Indian Wars," the federal government began a campaign to assimilate the American Indian into the dominant culture. American Indians were not made citizens of the United States until 1924. Within this setting, American Indian children were sent to boarding schools, beginning in 1870 and not ending until the 1950s. The concept of the boarding school was that through a Western education, the American Indians would forget their own heritage and language and adopt the dominant culture's values, beliefs, and cultural mores. The boarding school was a disaster, and the ill effects continue to plague the American Indian population through a cultural phenomenon known as "multigenerational grief."

The history of the government's treatment of the American Indians is not a positive one. A history of the federal government's broken promises includes the breaking of all treaties signed with the federal government. The boarding schools, broken treaties, current issues with casinos, water rights, land management, and repatriation of sacred artifacts and ancestral remains afflict today's American Indian with any awareness of their tribal government's relationships with federal/state entities. Lastly, the assault on spiritual ceremonies and practices continues today.

Closer to home, this problem exists in today's corrections system. This total lack of understanding and often, respect for American Indian's spiritual beliefs and practices, has created fertile ground for an ethnic community that feels misunderstood, disenfranchised, and powerless.

The American Indian working within the corrections system may be seen through a cultural continuum that covers a spectrum of traditional beliefs and practices to one fully assimilated within mainstream America. The corrections officer with an Indian heritage or background may be an elusive candidate for stereotyping or the person could proudly assume his or her history and background from their ethnic group. There are, however, some universal areas wherein all American Indians share similarities.

When one works directly or indirectly with an American Indian corrections officer, an appropriate question to ask that is not disrespectful or intrusive is one's tribal affiliation. With more than 525 federally recognized tribes, the stereotypical response is to overlook this important aspect of Indian identity. Tribal membership is something in which every American Indian takes extreme pride—being a recognized member of his or her specific tribe. This is important to Indian identity.

Another question that may be asked after tribal identity is established is: Were you raised on a reservation or in an urban setting? Reservation life is equally good and harsh. The connectedness that individuals feel to their home reservation is important to the individuals' sense of belonging. Equally, one could have been raised in an urban setting and may have a different response to this question. Whatever the question, it tells the respondent that you have taken the time to learn and respect some aspects of the American Indian's way of life. Even with this small degree of knowledge, the respondent should feel complimented by your questions, not intruded upon.

There are many more areas of "Indianness" that define native cultural identity. These include, but are not limited to, the following: tribal language, an Indian name, participation in traditional ceremonies, spiritual practices, and beliefs. These life areas are extremely private and may be revealed based on the degree of trust that develops between coworkers. There are areas within culture where information is never to be shared. Sacred ceremonies, songs, rituals, and prayers are determined to be private by the tribe of origin. Therefore, fellow employees should not feel put off or mistrusted if they do not share certain information.

The American Indian in today's work environment may appear quiet and reserved or may be gregarious and outgoing. There is no concrete definition for personalities or behaviors that may differ from the dominant culture. The most important aspect to keep in mind may be that today's American Indian is much like anyone else. The stereotype of feathers and beads or the "noble savage" are compartments in which the dominant society finds easiest to put the American Indian. This view is prejudicial, rigid, and damaging to professional and personal interactions and creates suspicion and mistrust.

A final watchword for any workforce that contains diversity in ethnicity, beliefs, and/or cultural backgrounds is respect. This means respect for a fellow worker's beliefs and backgrounds that may differ from one's own.

Suggested References for Further Reading and Viewing

Brown, Dee Alexander. 1991. *Bury My Heart at Wounded Knee: An Indian History of the American West*. New York: Henry Holt and Company.

Deloria, Vine, Jr., Leslie Marmon Silko, and George Tinker. 1969. *Custer Died for Your Sins: An Indian Manifesto*. New York: MacMillan Publishing.

———. 1972. *God Is Red: A Native View of Religion*. Golden, Colorado: Fulcrum Publishing.

Peltier, Leonard and Harvey Arden, eds. *Prison Writings: My Life Is My Sundance*. New York: St. Martin's Press.

Videos and DVDs:

Dance Me Outside. 1995. VHS. 84 minutes. Anchor Bay Entertainment, Troy, Michigan.

The Education of Littletree. 2001. 112 minutes. United International Pictures, San Pedro, California.

The Great Spirit within the Hole. 1983. 60 minutes. UNL Video Services.

Medicine River. 1997. United American Video.

Pow Wow Highway. 1998. 88 minutes. Anchor Bay Entertainment, Troy Michigan.

Smoke Signals. 1998. 89 minutes. Miramax Home Entertainment.

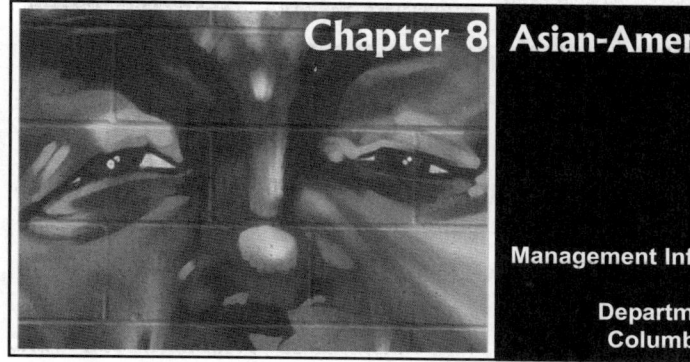

Chapter 8 Asian-Americans

Meesim C. Lee
Chief,
Management Information Services
South Carolina
Department of Corrections
Columbia, South Carolina

This author was honored and privileged to have been asked to contribute a chapter on Asian-American culture. She embarked on a journey of literature reading, statistics gathering, web surfing, memory jogging, and soul searching. It soon became apparent that she could not adequately and equitably address all peoples and cultures, classified categorically as "Asian-Americans." Voluminous facts, figures, and commentaries, did not, and could not, instantaneously transform her into a cultural diversity scholar, or an expert in the specific cultures of fellow Asian-Americans, including those who share her Chinese ancestry. Neither could she completely discard her personal experiences and individual perspectives in her interpretation of what she read. She has spent thirty-one years, voluntarily, as an employee in the prison system in South Carolina, where only a meager 1.1 percent of its population is Asian-American.[1] In a small rural state, with few Asian-Americans and low immigration levels, cultural diversity issues and Asian-American interactions dwarf and pale in content, scale, and intensity, when compared with large states with major metropolitan areas, and higher concentrations of Asians.

This chapter tries to capture some common perceptions and myths; presents facts, figures, and references; and provides readers with a glimpse of Asian-American communities and their viewpoints. As an introduction to Asian-Americans and their culture in general, this chapter aims at promoting awareness, and should not be construed to be golden rules to classify individuals and/or guide behavior. Stereotyping, in any degree, based on the limited information in this chapter, will defeat the very purpose of this publication. All of us, irrespective of race, ancestry, or ethnicity, deserve to be treated as individuals.

Asian-American Encounters

Scene 1: The Foreigner

Setting: An overcrowded cafeteria, department of corrections headquarters, noon, a rainy day in September, 1999.

Jim Brown, a new hire in construction, managed to find an empty seat at the table, where Mary Chin, a ten-year department of corrections veteran in research was finishing her salad. After self-introductions, pleasantries on the weather, and comments on the quality of cafeteria food, Jim asked, "Mary, what nationality are you?"

"American," Mary replied.

Jim shook his head gently, "I mean, where do you come from?"

Mary smiled and said, "Memphis, Tennessee."

"Well . . . I mean, did you come from China, Korea, or Japan?"

Mary nodded, "I see." She added, "I am American born and bred. Not a foreigner. If you want to know my roots, then, my great-great-grandfather left China many, many years ago. He worked on the Pacific Railroad."

Sheepishly and apologetically, Jim uttered, "I didn't mean to come across that way."

"It's alright, I can handle that." Mary held her smile and thought to herself, "Well, you are not the first, and will certainly not be the last."

Scene 2: The Karate Kid

Setting: Department of corrections cafeteria, noon, March 26,

2001. The night before, *Crouching Tiger Hidden Dragon* won the Best Foreign Film award in the Oscar ceremony.

Jim Brown noticed Mary Chin in the lunchroom, and went over to join her.

"Hi, long time no see, Mary. I see we're both still stuck here. Not paroled yet?"

"Nope. How have you been?" Mary replied.

"So, so," Jim murmured. Then, his eyes lit up, and enthusiastically, he asked, "Oh, Mary, maybe you can help. My kid was roughed up in school a little, and I want him to learn Karate, and the Kung Fu bit— like those characters in *Crouching Tiger Hidden Dragon*. You must know someone who is good in that."

"Jim, I am honored that you asked. But frankly, I don't. Not all Asian-Americans are into martial arts and can fight like Bruce Lee."

Scene 3: The Mistaken Identity

Setting: Same overcrowded cafeteria, department of corrections headquarters, a dreary day, September 16, 2001. At the lunch table where Mary Chin and Jim Brown sat, employees were updating one another on the latest developments on the World Trade Center and September 11. The day before, two Sikhs, mistaken to be Middle Eastern men, were murdered. Yusef Khan, a computer consultant came in to the cafeteria with a food tray, and Mary Chin waved at him, gesturing for him to come over.

"Hey, Mary, who is he? Is he Middle Eastern? Are you sure you want him to join us?" Jim asked apprehensively.

"Don't worry. Yusef is American, though he has Pakistani roots." Mary replied.

"But he is Muslim. Now, we all have to shut up." Jim uttered with disgust.

"Come on, Jim, you are wrong again. Yusef is Christian. Just like you, he reads the Bible and goes to church every Sunday. He is as much a victim in this nightmare as we all are."

89

The Asian-American Myth—Perception versus Reality

The three Asian-American encounters are snapshots of reality, although the characters' names are fictitious to respect the privacy of the individuals. They illustrate how people act and respond according to their perceptions or preconceived notions, which may represent truths, half-truths, or untruths. Jim Brown's questions in the first two episodes, whether driven by curiosity or intended to be sociable, most likely stemmed from his preconceived notions that (1) all Asian-looking persons are foreigners or new immigrants, and (2) all Asians are the same.

In her spontaneous reflex answers, Mary Chin responded, not so much to Jim Brown, but to these generalizations and assumptions, frequently discussed in contemporary Asian-American commentaries and literature. To Mary, and many Asian-Americans born and raised in the United States and entrenched in mainstream culture, a nonresponse or less challenging response would imply abandoning their birthrights and citizenship, an unpatriotic act indeed. In the third episode, like the majority of Americans jolted by September 11 and its aftermath, Jim Brown could not help his misgivings; assuming that all East Asian-Americans follow Islam, and all followers of Islam hate America.

Are all Asian-Americans Foreigners?

It is not difficult to appreciate why many Americans think that all or nearly all Asian-Americans are foreigners. Asian-Americans differ in physical appearance from mainstream Americans. American history in the classroom does not have a place for Asian-Americans, since they were engaged in few milestone events that shaped this nation. "Asian-Americans" is a relatively new term to denote race, ethnicity, and ancestry, more familiar to census statisticians and politicians running for office than to the general public.

Traditionally, Americans of Asian origin were identified by the individual countries from which they originally migrated (Chinese,

Koreans, Filipino, Vietnamese, Indian, and so forth), thus, making it easy and convenient to align them to a foreign country other than the United States. Even after three decades of dramatic increase in count, Asian-Americans constitute only 4.2 percent of the current population in the United States, and over half (51 percent) live in just three states: California, New York, and Hawaii.[2]

Asian-Americans rarely appeared in national headlines until, at the turn of the new millennium, the sensationalism of alleged spying and the horror of September 11 hit home for every American household. In 1999, fifty-nine charges of spying and espionage were brought against Dr. Wen Ho Lee, a naturalized American scientist working for the U.S. Department of Energy at its laboratory in Los Alamos, New Mexico. In September 2000, all charges except one were dropped, and Dr. Lee was released after pleading guilty to one count of mishandling computer data. On September 15, 2001, four days after September 11, two Sikhs were mistaken to be Arabs and murdered. In airports, selected Pakistani and East-Indian Americans were removed from airplanes. When national security is at stake, who is to blame for doubting the citizenship or loyalty of foreign looking Asian-Americans?

Tempting and logical as it seems to justify this stereotyping of Asian-Americans, we should also come to terms with realities. Based on various Bureau of Census' reports, this author estimated that among Asian-Americans, up to 4.6 million were native-born U.S. citizens and 3.4 million were naturalized citizens. Combining citizenship by birth and by naturalization thus yields an estimated total of up to 8 million U.S. citizens among Asian-Americans—two out of every three Asian-Americans.

Are All Asian-Americans the Same?

It is not uncommon that we stereotype other people based on their appearances and from the perspective of our own knowledge and experience, no matter how limited or biased these may be. Here is an example of this author's own share of stereotyping. Before stepping on American soil and working for corrections, the term "American" evoked images of people like Katharine Hepburn and Cary Grant in *The Philadelphia Story*—well dressed, living in gorgeous homes, and driving fancy cars. Accordingly, just as easily and/or unconsciously, martial arts movie fans of Bruce Lee or Jackie Chan assume that fistfights and sidekicks are a way of life for Asian-American men. Similarly, it is not surprising that, based on their experience in Vietnam, some veterans were tempted to dismiss Asian-American women as imports from the streets of Saigon, thus unable to treat them as peers of equal standing in the workplace.

By nature of origin or definition according to the U.S. Census Bureau, Asian-Americans are anything but alike. According to the Census Bureau, "The term 'Asian' refers to people having origins in any of the original peoples of the Far East, Southeast Asia, or the Indian sub-continent (for example, Cambodia, China, India, Japan, Korea, Malaysia, Pakistan, the Philippine Islands, Thailand, and Vietnam). Asian groups are not limited to nationalities, but include ethnic terms, as well."[3] The Census Bureau also states that "The Asian population includes many groups who differ in language, culture, and length of residence in the United States. Some of the Asian groups, such as the Chinese and Japanese, have been in the United States for several generations. Other groups, such as the Hmong, Vietnamese, Laotians, and Cambodians, are comparatively recent immigrants."[3]

Furthermore, as immigrants assimilate with American main-stream, but in varying degrees, their socioeconomic status and cultural/political outlook became even more divergent. Some facts and figures are compiled to shed light on the diversity of Asian-Americans as a group of people, with their cultures as a conglomerate of some very different traditions and beliefs.

Asian-Americans—Some Facts and Figures

Counts: Fast Growing Minority Group

According to the U.S. Census Bureau, in the 2000 Census, about 11.9 million persons identified themselves as at least part Asian. Among them, 10.2 million reported themselves to be only Asians and 1.7 million people reported Asian and one or more other races. The 11.9 million persons represented 4.2 percent of the total population of 281.4 million in the United States in 2000. Based on the 1990 census count of 6.9 million Asians, from 1990 to 2000, the range for the increase in the Asian population was 48 percent to 72 percent (depending if the Asian alone or the combination population count of Asians is used in the computation).[4] This high rate of growth originated from the 1965 Immigration Act, which initiated provisions to allow American citizens, and in some cases, permanent residents, to petition for their family members to unite with them in America. Persons with exceptional professional skills or performing jobs in areas with documented labor shortages also can migrate to the United States. This change in immigration policy has opened the doors for many Asian-American immigrants in the last three decades and accounted for the large increase in the numbers of Asian-Americans.

Location: Concentration in the West and Coastal/Urban Areas

According to the 2000 Census, over half (51 percent) of the Asian population lived in just three states: California, New York, and Hawaii. California had the largest number of Asians (4.2 million), which was followed by New York (1.2 million), and Hawaii (0.7 million). Besides concentration in a few states, Asian-Americans also converge in coastal and/or urban areas. The two urban areas with the largest count of Asian-Americans were New York (872,777) and Los Angeles (407,444). The density of Asian-Americans in a geographical area may affect the manner in which they interact with one another and with non-Asian-Americans outside their communities. In the West, where almost one out of ten residents (9.3 percent) are Asian-American, familiarity or comfort level with Asian-American culture and communities will certainly differ from those in the prevalently rural South and Midwest, where only 2 out of 100 citizens are Asian-Americans (2.3 percent and 2.2 percent, respectively). In the Northeast, 4.4 percent of the total population is Asian-American.[5]

Geographic Origin

The U.S. Census identified more than twenty-four countries of origin for individuals who reported the race category of "Asian." While many countries are represented, China, the Philippines, India, Korea, Vietnam, and Japan comprise almost 90 percent of the Asian-American population.

Table 1: Asian Population by Detailed Group: 2000

(For information on confidentiality protection, nonsampling error, and definitions, see www.census.gov/prod/cen2000/docs/sf1.pdf)

Detailed Group	Asian Alone		Asian in Combination With One or More Other		Asian Detailed group alone or in any combination
	One Asian Group reported[1]	Two or more Asian Group	One Asian Group reported[1]	Two or more Asian Group reported[2]	
Total	**10,019,405**	**223,593**	**1,516,841**	**138,989**	**11,898,828**
Asian Indian	1,678,765	40,013	165,437	15,384	1,899,599
Bangladeshi	41,280	5,625	9,655	852	57,412
Bhutanese	183	9	17	3	212
Burmese	13,159	1,461	1,837	263	16,720
Cambodian	171,937	11,832	20,830	1,453	206,052
Chinese, except Taiwanese	2,314,537	130,826	201,688	87,790	2,734,841
Filipino	1,850,314	57,811	385,236	71,454	2,364,815
Hmong	169,428	5,284	11,153	445	186,310
Indo Chinese	113	55	23	8	199
Indonesian	39,757	4,429	17,256	1,631	63,073
Iwo Jiman	15	3	60	-	78
Japanese	796,700	55,537	241,209	55,486	1,148,932
Korean	1,076,872	22,550	114,211	14,794	1,228,427
Laotian	168,707	10,396	17,914	1,186	198,203
Malaysian	10,690	4,339	2,837	700	18,566
Maldivian	27	2	22	-	51
Neaplese	7,858	351	1,128	62	9,399
Okinawan	3,513	2,625	2,816	1,645	10,599
Pakistani	153,533	11,095	37,587	2,094	204,309
Singaporean	1,437	580	307	70	2,394
Sri Lankan	20,145	1,219	2,966	257	24,587
Taiwanese	118,048	14,096	11,394	1,257	144,795
Thai	112,989	7,929	27,170	2,195	150,283
Vietnamese	1,122,528	47,144	48,639	5,425	1,233,736
Other Asian, not specified[6]	146,870	19,576	195,449	7,535	369,430

Diverse Cultural Background—Language, Religion, and Customs

Embodied in a people's culture are their languages, religions, values, norms, philosophy, customs, and etiquette—in short, a way of life. By their varied geographic origin and ancestry, Asian-American cultures are extremely diverse. While some differences are well recognized by mainstream America, very often, subtle uniqueness is only noticeable or noted by individual subgroups within Asian-American communities.

While the Census listed twenty-four major countries of origin, the Commission on Asian Pacific Americans (Washington State) identified sixty-six dialects spoken in Asian-American communities—including eleven dialects among Chinese-Americans, and three spoken on the Indian subcontinent.

Besides language differences, the ancestral countries of Asian-Americans were also distinguished by the unique religions of their people. A tally of the religions practiced in these countries illustrates the variations in religious beliefs, and related customs and traditions, among Asian-Americans in this country. Citing the 2000 *CIA World Fact Book,* Cuong Ngugen Le listed the religious proportions of various Asian countries in his web site, Asian Nation (www.asian-nation.org). Mr. Le, a research associate at the Center for Technology and Government, State University of New York at Albany, developed his web site to be a "one-stop information sources on the historical, political, social, economic, and cultural elements and issues that make up today's diverse Asian community."

For example, in the Philippines, 83 percent of the population is Catholic, followed by Protestants (9 percent), Muslim (5 percent), and Buddhist or other religion (3 percent). Similarly, by its French colonialism history, there is a large Catholic following in Vietnam. While Muslims are the majority in Bangladesh (88 percent), they are the minority in India (14 percent). On the other hand, while Hindus are in the minority (10.5 percent) in Bangladesh, they are the predominant religion in India (80 percent). In Japan 84 percent of the population observe both Shinto and Buddhist religions. In South Korea, about half (49 percent) of the population is Christian.[7] As a contrast, while some Chinese are Catholics, Protestants, or Buddhists, the majority of them do not have a religious affiliation, but rather observe ceremonies to show respect for their ancestors.

Just as varied as their religious beliefs, Asian-Americans arrived in the United States by different paths over different periods in American history. Each group's experience reflected the various U.S. immigration laws, the need for labor, either physical or intellectual, and each group's socioeconomic composition. While the earliest wave of Asian-Americans came to the United States as laborers working on farms and railroad construction, many Asian-Americans arriving in the United States after 1965, pursuant to the liberalization of immigration laws, were professionals, scientists, engineers, and business people, with diverse and very different socio-economic and cultural backgrounds.

In summary, U.S. immigration laws remained exclusionary against Asians until 1965 when, in response to the civil rights movement, non-restrictive annual quotas of 20,000 immigrants per country were established. For the first time in U.S. history, large numbers of Asians were able to come to the United States as families. In addition, due to the Untied States' eagerness for technology during the Cold War, foreign engineers and scientists were encouraged to immigrate to the United States. In the last three decades, pursuant to the liberalization of immigration laws in 1965, Asian-Americans of diverse cultural, religious, and socioeconomic backgrounds became an integral part of American society.

Evolving Culture among Asian-Americans

Perhaps, the author's personal perspective or experiences may help to illustrate or emphasize the evolving nature and generational differences of Asian cultures or Asian-American ways of life. Confucian tenets, dominant in traditional Chinese literature and history, submit the individual to the family and social structure, emphasize filial piety and obedience, dictate respect for "older" people, instruct women to follow their fathers, husbands, and sons, and frown on physical contact between men and women in public. From the author's early indoctrination in that philosophy, growing up in Hong Kong, then a British colony, she always addressed her superiors formally, and it took years of transitioning into American society to be able to address "older" people by their first name. Similarly, it took some time and psychological conditioning to get used to friendly hugs and embraces. Would this personal perspective have been interpreted as being respectful or being aloof and unfriendly in the workplace? Since Confucian teaching was deemphasized during the cultural revolution in China, and China has opened its doors to the West for over two decades, she cannot address to what degree Confucian teaching would have been entrenched among first-generation immigrants from that country.

While many Asian-Americans of an older generation were expected to follow their parents' wishes, including whom they were arranged to marry, she was exempted from such practice because of her Western education and exposure. It is natural from their upbringing in American society that Asian-Americans of the younger generation would find such arrangements repulsive, an intrusion into their individualism, and a violation of their civil rights. Similarly, the majority of contemporary Asian-American women will certainly not accept the idea that a woman's virtue is measured by her subordination to her immediate male family members.

Researching and contemplating for this chapter, she cannot escape from an analysis of her own way of life—how much is it traditional or contemporary Chinese, Asian or American, or how representative she is of Asian-Americans in general. She can only conclude that, to understand and interact with a person, whether in or outside of the workplace, we must transcend the limits of our own individual cultures or experiences, steer away from casting another person in the confines of his or her ancestral or geographic roots; and above all, recognize that an individual's values, beliefs, and behavior are products of unique personalities and backgrounds.

Asian-Americans in the Criminal Justice System

Relatively few Asian-Americans are engaged in the criminal justice system as employees or as offenders. Because of their small numbers, the Bureau of Justice Statistics (BJS) reported Asian-American employment in a category of "other races" (along with American Indians, Alaska Natives, and Pacific Islanders), and grouped Asians and Pacific Islanders together in criminal justice system population reports. By the latest statistical reports available from the Bureau of Justice Statistics, there were 6,576 (1.9 percent) persons of other races employed (in any capacity) in state correctional facilities across the nation in 1995.[8] Among them, 6,422 were employed as correctional officers. Considering that most likely Pacific Islanders would comprise a significant number among this group, by their employment in the Hawaiian criminal justice system, it is reasonable to assume that Asian-American employment in correctional systems is significantly lower than their 4 percent representation in the general U.S. population.

Similarly, Asian-Americans are substantially lower in counts and proportion among persons incarcerated in prisons or supervised under parole or probation. The Bureau of Justice Statistics reported a total of 1,364,897 persons were incarcerated in the nation's prisons on December 31, 1999. Among them, 7,443 were reported to be Asian-Americans and 2,362 were Pacific Islanders. These represented 0.5 percent and 0.2 percent, respectively of the nation's prisoner population.

A review of the Bureau of Justice Statistics' probation and parole population data on race concludes that information is too incomplete for any meaningful interpretation of Asian-American population on probation and parole. To illustrate, California reported 3,098 and 3,213 parolees with unknown/not reported race in 1990 and 2000, respectively. Some of the states that did not report race for their entire parole population in 2000 were Hawaii, New Jersey, Indiana, Kentucky, and New Mexico. Similarly in probation statistics reported by the Bureau of Justice Statistics, some of the states that did not report race for their entire probation population were California, Illinois, Indiana, Kansas, Massachusetts, Rhode Island, and New Mexico.

Conclusion

Rather than itemizing specifics of Asian-American culture, this chapter offers some personal perspectives and viewpoints relating to Asian-Americans and/or Asian-American culture. These discussions, however, are not intended to instruct readers on what to do or not to do in the work place or correctional setting, when interacting with Asian-American colleagues or clients. It is hoped that by portraying the dynamic and adaptive nature of culture and emphasizing people as individuals, readers will better appreciate the diversity of Asian-Americans in the complexities of their culture. For those readers interested in more information on specific topics or issues relating to Asian-American communities and their culture, the bibliography in this chapter contains references and web site addresses to facilitate research.

Notes

[1] Jessica S. Barnes and Claudette E. Bennett. February 2002. "The Asian Population: 2000," *Census 2000 Brief*, C2KBR/01-16 (Washington, D.C.: U.S. Department of Commerce, Economics and Statistics Administration, Bureau of Census), Table 2: Asian Population for the United States, Regions, and States, and for Puerto Rico: 1990 and 2000, p. 5. Available: http://www.census.gov/prod/2002pubs/ c2kbr01-16.pdf.

[2] Barnes and Bennett, p. 1 and p. 4.

[3] Barnes and Bennett, Footnote 1, p. 1.

[4] Barnes and Bennett, p. 1 and p. 3.

[5] Barnes and Bennett, p. 4.

[6] Barnes and Bennett, p. 1.

[7] "Religion, Spirituality, and Faith," (n.d.), Asian Nation. Available: http://www.asian-nation.org/ culture.html.

[8] James J. Stephan, August 1997, "Census of State and Federal Correctional Facilities, 1995," *Executive Summary*, NCJ 166582 (Washington, D.C.: U.S. Department of Justice, Office of Justice Programs, Bureau of Justice Statistics), p. 3. Available: http://www.ojp.usdoj.gov/bjs/pub/pdf/ csfc95ex.pdf.

References

APA Demographics. (n.d.). *Commission on Asian Pacific American Affairs (Washington State)*. Available: http://www.capaa.wa.gov/community.html. [Accessed: 4 June 2002].

Barnes, Jessica S. and Claudette E Bennet. February 2002. The Asian Population: 2000. *Census 2000 Brief*. C2KBR/01-16. Washington, D.C.: U.S. Department of Commerce, Economics and Statistics Administration, Bureau of Census. Available: http://www.census.gov/ prod/2002pubs/c2kbr01-16.pdf [Accessed: 26 July 2002].

Bureau of Census. 1990. Profiles of General Demographic Characteristics: 1990. *1990 Census of Population and Housing*. Washington, D.C.: U.S. Department of Commerce, Economics and Statistics Administration. Available: http://www.census.gov/Press-Release/www/ 2001/tables/dp_us_1990.PDF. [Accessed: 29 July 2002].

———. 2001. Section 1: Population. *Statistical Abstract of the United States: 2001*. Washington, D.C.: U.S. Department of Commerce, Economics and Statistics Administration. Available: http://www.census.gov/prod/2002pubs/01statab/pop.

pdf. [Accessed: 30 July 2002].

————. May 2001. Profiles of General Demographic Characteristics: 2000. *2000 Census of Population and Housing.* Washington, D.C.: U.S. Department of Commerce, Economics and Statistics Administration. Available: http://www.census.gov/prod/cen2000/dp1/2kh00.pdf. [Accessed: 29 July 2002].

————. May 2001. Asian Pacific American Month: May 1-31. *Census Bureau Facts for Features. CB01-FF.06.* Washington, D.C.: U.S. Department of Commerce, Economics and Statistics Administration. Available http://www.census.gov/Press-Release/www/2001/cb01ff06.html. [Accessed: 12 August 2002].

————. June 2001. Nation's Asian and Pacific Islander Population Profiled by Census Bureau. *United States Department of Commerce News.* CB01-111. Washington, D.C.: U.S. Department of Commerce, Economics and Statistics Administration. Available http://www.census.gov/Press-Release/www/2001/cb01-111.html. [Accessed: 12 August 2002].

————. February 2002. *Profile of the Foreign-born Population in the United States, 2000.* PPL-145. Washington, D.C.: U.S. Department of Commerce, Economics and Statistics Administration. Available: http://www.census.gov/population/socdemo/foreign/ppl-145/tab07-1.pdf. [Accessed: 26 July 2002].

Bureau of Justice Statistics. 1984. *Census of State Correctional Facilities.* Washington, D.C.: U.S. Department of Justice, Office of Justice Programs. June 30.

————. June 1990. *Census of State and Federal Correctional Facilities, 1990.* Washington, D.C.: U.S. Department of Justice, Office of Justice Programs.

————. Midyear 1995. *Census of State and Federal Correctional Facilities, 1995.* Washington, D.C.: U.S. Department of Justice, Office of Justice Programs.

————. 2000. *Correctional Populations in the United States, 1999.* Washington, D.C.: U.S. Department of Justice, Office of Justice Programs.

Bustillo, Miebeth. February-April 2002. *Preserving Our Civil Rights During National Crises.* Commission on Asian Pacific American Affairs (Washington State) Vol. 2(4), p. 5. Available: http://www.capaa.wa.gov/pdf/2002v2i4.pdf. [Accessed: 24 July 2002].

Chepesiuk, Ron. 2001. Asian America Has Bloomed—Will U.S. Companies Notice? *Asian Week.* March 23-29. Available: http://www.asianweek.com/2001_03_23 /section_business.html. [Accessed: 23 July 2002].

Commission on Asian Pacific American Affairs: Overview. (n.d.). *Commission on Asian Pacific American Affairs (Washington State).* Available: http://www.capaa.wa.gov/about.html. [Accessed: 23 July 2002].

Eggen, Dan. 2001. Report Details More FBI Blunders in Wen Ho Lee Probe. *Washington Post,* August 27, A1. Available: http://www.washingtonpost.com/ac2/wp-dyn?pagename=article&node =&contentId=A623-2001Aug26. [Accessed: 23 July 2002].

Huang, Gary. December 1993. *Beyond Culture: Communicating with Asian American Children and Families.* ERIC, ED366673. Available: http://www.ed.gov/databases/ERIC_Digests/ed366673.html. [Accessed: 23 July 2002].

Jankowski, Louis W. July 1992. *Correctional Populations in the United States, 1990.* NCJ-134946. Washington, D.C.: U.S. Department of Commerce, Economics and Statistics Administration, Bureau of Census.

Koritala, Srirajasekhar B. (n.d.). *A Historical Perspective of Americans of Asian Indian Origin 1790–1997.* Available: http://www.infinityfoundation.com/mandala/h_es/h_es_korit_histical.htm. [Accessed: 23 July 2002].

Koseki, Lawrence K. 1993. Asian Americans and Pacific Islanders: Minorities within a Minority. *Understanding Cultural Diversity*. Lanham, Maryland: American Correctional Association.

Minato, Ryan. November 2000. South Asian Americans. *Commission on Asian Pacific American Affairs (Washington State)*. Vol. 1(4), p. 1. Available: http://www.capaa.wa. gov/pdf/ November2000v1i4.pdf. [Accessed: 23 July 2002].

————. July-September 2001. Japanese Americans. *Commission on Asian Pacific American Affairs (Washington State)*. Vol. 2(2), p. 4. Available: http://www.capaa. wa.gov/pdf/2001v2i2.pdf. [Accessed: 24 July 2002].

————. Winter 2001. Filipino Americans. *Commission on Asian Pacific American Affairs (Washington State)*. Vol. 2(1), p. 4. Available: http://www.capaa.wa.gov/pdf/ Winter2001v2i1.pdf. [Accessed: 23 July 2002].

————. October-December 2001. Chinese Americans. *Commission on Asian Pacific American Affairs (Washington State)*. Vol. 2(3), p. 4. Available: http://www.capaa. wa.gov/pdf/2001v2i3.pdf. [Accessed: 23 July 2002].

————. February-April 2002. Vietnamese Americans. *Commission on Asian Pacific American Affairs (Washington State)*. Vol. 2(4), p. 4. Available: http://www.capaa.wa. gov/pdf/2002v2i4.pdf. [Accessed: 24 July 2002].

Minato, Ryan and Miebeth R. Bustillo-Hutchins. September 2000. Korean Americans. *Commission on Asian Pacific American Affairs (Washington State)*. Vol. 1(3), p. 4. Available: http://www.capaa.wa.gov/pdf/September2000v1i3.pdf. [Accessed: 24 July 2002].

Religion, Spirituality, and Faith. (n.d). *Asian Nation*. Available: http://www.asian-nation.org/culture.html. [Accessed: 31 July 2002].

Rocher, Rosane. Spring 1995. South Asian American Studies: A Working Bibliography 1975-1994. *South Asia Graduate Research Journal (SAGAR)*. Vol. 2(1). Available from University of Texas at Austin, Center for Asian Studies website: http://asnic. utexas.edu/asnic/pages/ sagar/spring.1995/ rosane.rocher.spr.95.html. [Accessed: 23 July 2002].

Selected Dates and Events of Asian Pacific American History. (n.d). *Commission on Asian Pacific American Affairs (Washington State)*. Available: http://www.capaa. wa.gov/timeline.html. [Accessed: 23 July 2002].

Stephan, James J. August 1997. *Census of State and Federal Correctional Facilities, 1995*. Executive Summary, NCJ 166582. Washington, D.C.: U.S. Department of Justice, Office of Justice Programs, Bureau of Justice Statistics. Available: http://www.ojp. usdoj.gov/bjs/pub/pdf/csfc95ex.pdf. [Accessed August 12, 2002].

Vang, Ko. May 2000. Southeast Asian in Washington State. *Commission on Asian Pacific American Affairs (Washington State)*. Inaugural Issue, Vol. 1(1), p. 4. Available: http://www.capaa.wa.gov/pdf/May2000v1i1.pdf. [Accessed: 24 July 2002].

———. July 2000. Pacific Islanders 101. *Commission on Asian Pacific American Affairs (Washington State)*. Vol. 1(2), p. 4. Available: http://www.capaa.wa.gov/ pdf/July2000v1i2.pdf. [Accessed: 23 July 2002].

Yin, Xiao-Huang. 2000. The Two Sides of America's Model Minority. *Los Angeles Times*. May 7. Available: http://modelminority.com/identity/twosides.htm. [Accessed: 31 May 2002].

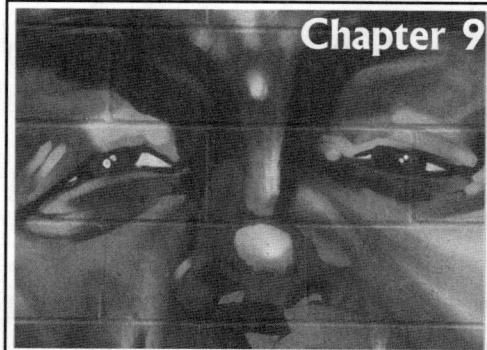

Chapter 9 African-American Women in Corrections

Mary V. Leftridge Byrd
Deputy Secretary
Pennsylvania Department
of Corrections
Camp Hill, Pennsylvania

Walking through the administration building lobby one morning, my eye was drawn to a group of young people sitting, chatting animatedly about the prospects of being escorted on tour through a state prison. The truth is, I was not certain what group they represented nor the college or university from which they hailed. I hadn't time to stop and ask as I was en route to new staff orientation. Walking into the training room, I looked and realized the same young people, those "students" were newly hired correctional officer trainees! This is likely the point at which I began to wonder to myself, as I met each new class of trainees, do their parents know they are in a prison this morning? This is also likely the moment I realized the steadily increasing number of young women entering the workforce, particularly as correctional officers.

My experience quickly led me to the reality that, for the most part, these young women had not had formative experiences that modeled how to be comfortable in the clothes of uniformed authority—especially in a closed environment built on a paramilitaristic model. I knew instinctively that aside from the required pre- and inservice regimen of training experience at the five-week residential academy, there would be another sphere of training these young staff would need to flatten a pathway toward achievement, success, individual satisfaction, and longevity.

Having entered the criminal justice field twenty plus years ago, I did not have the benefit of any coordinated nor structured training period and certainly had no women who modeled success simply because there were so few and rarely several in one jurisdiction. Compounding my individual challenge was the fact that there were few African-Americans and women (or African-American women) in positions as line, supervisory, and executive personnel. In fact, at one point I was the single woman parole agent in an urban field office and found myself in the constant company of majority males.

The same scenario repeated itself fifteen years later, when I became a prison superintendent. In each of these positions, it had been my reality that what was done well was overlooked and what was not done up to standard was magnified. This occurred in a world where too often mediocrity was the standard. It is this experience that helped me understand, in an intimate way, what the quote over the entranceway to a library on the campus of a traditionally black college intended. The quote cautions, "In order to be equal you must excel." Despite these hurdles, I did and continue to reach for the highest standards and work in a way that connects head and heart and decries unethical, racist, sexist, or other ugly behaviors.

For the most part, encouragement came from outside rather than within the professional arena, where the scarcity of persons who looked like me had a profound effect on my professional development. A number of realities I have witnessed and been subject to have helped me grow, and a number have forced me to grow. Obviously not all of these career chapters have been sweet nor do they bring fond memories. The single most important life lesson had been to make a pact with myself that when I reached a position that could be part of recruiting, hiring, retaining, training, teaching, and promoting women with a focus on the few women of color I had encountered on my career path, I would do just that. Surely shifting demographics as to the emerging workforce has given me the opportunity to breathe life into that pact.

Not long ago, some would have referred to the presence of women in corrections as a nuisance or even an oddity—perhaps too much of an oddity for any serious attention. Not unlike female offenders, the economies of scale doctrine seemingly fostered relative apathy or simple disregard for women in this arena.

As we have learned through research, personal account, and history, women had been relegated to working only with women offenders and inmates committed to institutions housing women. At that point, it may have been that the mindset was—who cared? Little mattered, as long as we were in the right and appropriate place for women. Our roles were narrowly defined by the perimeter of places of detention for wayward girls and loose women. Women working in corrections were virtually unheard of prior to the mid 1980s. In fact, our earlier sisters worked exclusively as matrons only supervising women (then and still now referred to in some quarters as "girls"). Given how resources were allocated, there is small wonder there was little focus on women working in this field.

It was not until the 1970s that any substantial change occurred as to the role of women particularly in institutional corrections. According to the U.S. Department of Labor, historically black women have had higher labor force participation rates than white and Hispanic women. Between 1994 and 1996, however, black and white women had virtually identical rates—approximately 59 percent and Hispanic women participated at a rate of about 53 percent. Since that time, black women have edged ahead with a participation rate of 63.5 percent in 1999. White and Hispanic women participated at 59.6 and 55.9 percent, respectively. Hispanic origin women are gradually narrowing the participation gap between themselves and their white counterparts (Facts on Women Workers by U.S. Department of Labor, Women's Bureau).

The increasing numbers of women working in criminal justice, reflecting these same changes nationally, can be attributed to a number of reasons:

- Enactment of civil rights legislation
- Welfare reform
- Changes in public assistance programs—nationally and locally
- National movements resulting in increasing consciousness around diversity and inclusion

According to the American Correctional Association's *2002 Directory Adult and Juvenile Correctional Departments, Institutions, Agencies, and Probation and Parole Authorities*, nationally, there were 36,121 African-American female correctional personnel as compared to 84,883 Caucasian females. These numbers obviously reflect a major difference and the same is true when African-American females are compared to Caucasian males who number 192,343. It is interesting to note the number of African-American males total 40,289, only 4,168 more than African-American females.

There are similar comparisons in juvenile justice agencies where 13,141 African-American females are employed as compared to 20,308 Caucasian females and 34,860 Caucasian males. Again, it is interesting to note the relatively slight difference in the number of African-American males—14,440; only a difference of 1,299 when compared with African-American females. The numbers of adult correctional administrators tells a striking story. There are more than three times as many Caucasian female administrators (3,902) as there were African-American administrators (1,163) and more than five times (5,510) the number of Caucasian male administrators. Relative to the largest classification of any correctional workforce, the number of African-American correctional officers who are female total 22,592 as compared to 27,289 Caucasian females. In the same classification, the number of Caucasian males total 127,285 and the pattern repeats itself relative to the parallel numbers of African-American males, which is 30,001. These numbers, their similarities, and differences have set up a dynamic backdrop for the emerging and historic culture of correctional organizations.

Considering the realities of traditional business organizations, which typically are constructed in the hierarchical model, it has been said that "his-tory" has demonstrated only part of the work world, how to do the work, and who should or can do the work. The power structure the nation has held up, if only by what has been routinely shown or demonstrated, is one that fails to effectively acknowledge the role of women in a way that suggests inclusiveness to be invaluable. What we know is that the U.S. presidency has not been held by a woman; that the authors of the U.S. Constitution were not women; that women in congressional bodies, though increasing, are clearly still seen as pioneers; that the original founders and leaders of religions have not, for the most part, been women; that world leaders, at least those we see on the nightly news, are men. These obvious examples of leadership may have an even greater impact on minority women than their counterparts given the similar dearth of African-American leaders in the field of corrections.

The challenges of corrections are often faced and managed differently—particularly by young African-American women who may find certain requirements confounding, unnecessary, or stilted. Chain of command, the expectation to "document, document, document," reporting in writing significant or atypical situations without question, and following the last order given can prove to be aggravating—especially to those who may be accustomed or acculturated to speak first, "cut to the chase," confront the issue quickly, or otherwise handle the events of life. Absent understanding or being given ample opportunity and explanation, these staff may find themselves on a short list leading toward corrective action, discipline, or separation from service. Employers, departments, supervisory staff, managerial personnel, and coworkers must begin to understand and make expectations clear, illuminating and honoring various life experiences and pathways new staff have traveled bringing them to a common place—at least a common place of employment.

With the now quickly changing demographics of our profession, there is an unusual and, indeed, unique opportunity to change the culture of corrections by maximizing and valuing the most important resources we have: our staff—all of them—even those who try our common sense. There must be the willingness to understand and have others understand that hiring a diverse staff is merely the beginning.

Change is a process, not an event. We must address the fact that corrections is a profession long on doing and short on planning. Leaders must ensure forecasting strategies are built around valuing human resources and inclusion as paramount guiding principles. All one need do is look at shifting demographics. According to the Urban League's *State of Black America*, by 2050, Caucasians will comprise only 53 percent of the nation's population. As these numbers change, so too will the number of women in the workforce. As was said in *Death of a Salesman*, attention must be paid.

Armed with the mantle of growing dissatisfaction of being relegated or invited to work only in facilities housing females and girded with the passage of amendment to the 1964 Civil Rights Act, women have pushed and in some cases litigated their way into positions and places formerly exclusively held by men. How women made room for themselves particularly in the 1970s left some sore souls.

This may have had an impact on women's assimilation or the acceptance of their presence, including their gifts and skills within the military model command structure of correctional institutions. Even considering the increased participation of women in the military, there is still a wide differentiation between those who do and do not appreciate the protocols and practices expected in the armed forces. Therefore, those who come to work in corrections who are not socialized to the military often find a challenge not experienced by their cohorts whose lives have exposed them to those attendant mores.

African-American women coming into corrections need to continue their self-development, parallel to the routine and mandatory preservice and inservice training provided by most correctional agencies.

An example is the expectation, based on duties and responsibilities, that a correctional officer candidate be proficient in and qualify for firearms training. It is likely a provable fact that women who are born to and raised in rural areas have access to weapons at a different rate than women born and raised in urban areas—where the majority of minority women live. Never mind the prevalence of gun violence in the country or the city, this is about having the opportunity to use weapons in a way that increases individual comfort level on a training range at a correctional academy.

Aside from becoming used to using varied weapons, in a very short period of time, a correctional officer trainee quickly must come to terms with the fact that continued employment is typically conditioned on weapons qualification. Firing ranges, which can be quite costly, may be the single opportunity for a trainee to practice when she is free on weekends during the academy training period. A trainee who returns to her rural home during free time likely has greatly unfettered opportunity to practice. This example is offered purely as a reality, not a crutch, and seeks to point out that the totality of circumstances should be considered, not in an effort to ease expectations but simply to provide another view of what this can mean for women new on the block.

Some believe that corrections remains the most sex-segregated and male-dominated stop along the criminal justice highway. The difference between tolerating or accepting women is for some exacerbated by the added element of ethnicity. Some staff may have the perception that an African-American woman staff member "knows" a number of inmates in the population; there may be the belief that she will not or cannot be objective because the officer and the inmate "come from the same place;" there may be the twisted assumption that most women must come to this work "looking for a man" and because institution populations are replete with men of color, surely she will have her pick, compromise herself (and therefore her peers), quit work, and live ever after with a former inmate.

In addressing staff during orientation, it is wise to address issues of sexism and racism found in the larger world and explore how these issues leech into and, in part, define institution culture. It is dangerous to pretend the esprit de corps found at terrific levels during preservice training, especially when the academy is residential, will continue to exist and be sustained at the same levels upon assignment to one's actual work site. Young women may misunderstand the attention and support given them by their peers during their preservice period of time.

Both early and often, it is smart to listen as new staff express what their own goals are and then determine how to help staff consider those goals against the backdrop of an institution's goals and objectives. Keys to advancement need to be stated, modeled, restated, and shown as having value relative to individual careers. Advancement can be articulated and achieved based on a number of guideposts to include:

- Making oneself known
- Improving individual skills
- Building a positive reputation
- Placing oneself correctly
- Avoiding mistakes
- Understanding the system
- Creating a forum to delineate, discuss, and review guiding principles

This last item pairs well with the more routine and necessary elements of orientation, initial training, and annual inservice training.

Among those principles, African-American women should be encouraged to stay tethered to something or someone real, both inside and outside of the correctional environment. Being "inside" for a protracted period of time can alter an individual's view of the world and how she fits. Additionally, these staff should be encouraged to understand the farther one ascends the ladder of achievement, the more exposed one's rear end becomes. The old adage about the same people one passes on the way up will be the same folks she passes as she falls from grace is an important lesson to teach. That one must be brilliant and humble should be an expected part of how one navigates the often choppy water that can course through and surround this world. It must be taught and modeled so that at the end of the day, she realizes that she has done her best and she must go home and await the results in peace.

It is critical that aside from CPR, defensive tactics, use of force, and sexual harassment training, we are teaching that adoption of masculine traits are not necessary for women to be assimilated but that professional traits are what are important. We must teach that challenging the process brings risk and that the most valuable things are gained with a (sometimes palpable) level of risk. These staff should understand that positions are transient, but character is forever. As a role model, help staff understand a title is not who one is—it merely defines what one does. Post orders, handcuffs, key rings, drug interdiction dogs, and search teams are important supports for the work but what is most important is how one demonstrates her integrity, impartiality, compassion, insight, and operational smarts. These are the things that more significantly speak to success. If a staff member has to state that she is in charge, she is not in charge of anything, least of all herself. It is absolutely critical to say and model in a number of ways how one achieves and sustains her success. This modeling is as important as the actual achievement.

Undeniably, there are challenges. Those in leadership, on all levels of an organization should confront and address these challenges. How we lead through those challenges is what needs to be internalized. Because our staff come to their work and responsibilities from so many avenues, we must see and celebrate the strength in diversity but not make an effort to blend their experiences. Instead, we must learn to weave the distinct, colorful, and sturdy threads to create the quilt that heralds a rich workforce. When we do not allow for differences, we say in subtle and obvious ways that staff who have all looked out of the same windows create a one-dimensional workforce that may only be equipped to deal in one way with the edginess often felt in correctional facilities. Equal parts of integrity, intellect, and creativity make for a dynamic organization.

The author issued the following list of touchstones to all staff, but it was conceived in response to the emergence of culture clashes among certain staff; a rub most often falling along the lines of gender and ethnicity. The object was to create a document built on common ground that would engender dialog toward understanding that though there appear to be vast differences, we can find commonality. Concurrently, we made an effort to provide guideposts that would be most useful to younger staff who may not yet have embraced correc- tions as a career. Perhaps these touchstones would be of use to others.

- I am more responsible than anyone else or anyplace else for my place in the universe.
- Do not seek permission, step out on faith and training.
- Wear comfortable shoes. Size six pumps will hurt more than any size wingtip ever intended.
- Begin with the end in mind.
- Strut your stuff—humbly.
- Every sister (or brother) ain't a sister (or brother).
- Do not abet the "isms."
- Define who you are by who you are not by what you do or your title.
- Distinguish yourself.
- Exercise key, tool, and self-control.
- Know the difference between your professional and personal boundaries—make this distinction clear.
- Work is not the place to satisfy personal needs.
- Feeling sorry for an inmate is not helpful nor is it smart.
- Be constantly aware of your own feelings.
- Conduct all interactions on the basis of mutual respect.

- Your departmental code of ethics is a dynamic reference document not a coaster.
- If something sounded off key or peculiar, it likely is.
- Each one teach one.
- Positive prejudice toward one person is negative prejudice toward another.
- We do not work for inmates—we work with them.
- There is no such thing as "my" inmate. If you find an inmate to be indispensable, something is broken.
- Never say anything, nor do anything you would not want your mama, a news reporter, your spouse, or your children to see, know, or hear.

There is no science to dealing with our staff; it is more nearly an art. In any case, few "rules" can or should be applied in a way that suggests formulae that have worked in the past will always work in the future. The convergence of public expectation, responsibilities of corrections professionals, and demand of the correctional environment, coupled with the cultural influence of the larger world, creates incredible dynamics. For those who work with the staff on the block, it is critical that benchmarks are established, standards set, and stops pulled out.

Circle of Stones

How might your life be different if there had been a place for you? A place of women, where you were received and affirmed. A place where other women, perhaps somewhat older, had been affirmed before you, each in her own time, affirmed, as she struggled to become more truly herself. A place where, after the fires were lighted, and the silence, there would be a hush of expectancy filling the entire chamber. A knowing that each woman there was leaving old conformity to find herself a sense that all of womanhood stood on a threshold. And if, during the hush, the other women, slightly older, had helped you to trust your own becoming to trust it and quietly and prayerfully to nurture it. How might your life be different?

Judith Duerk

Reprinted with permission from *Circle of Stones* by Judith Duerk.

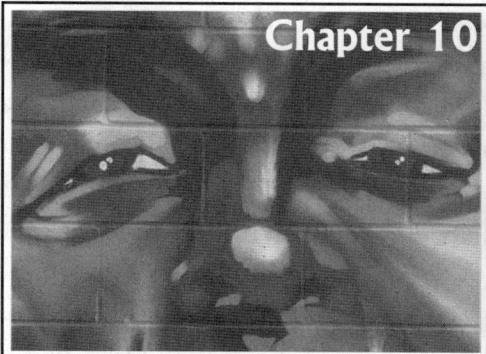

Chapter 10 Diversity in Correctional Management: An Essential Tool

Reginald A. Wilkinson, Ed.D.
Director,
Ohio Department of Rehabilitation
and Correction
Columbus, Ohio

Corrections, unlike many other occupations, is a field of work dealing with freedom and liberty, life and death. Like it or not, corrections leaders hold the daily quality of life for thousands of individuals in their hands. These offenders, whether incarcerated or under community supervision, are an incredibly diverse population. To manage this population effectively and humanely, with a goal of successful reentry into our society topmost in our minds, we must acknowledge and work with this human diversity.

With the breakup of the Soviet Union, the United States, according to the International Center for Prison Studies, now holds the dubious distinction of incarcerating the most people, per capita. The people we supervise are young and old; male and female; and black, white, Hispanic, Native American, Arabic, and Asian. They come from myriad backgrounds and cultures—Appalachian, Caribbean, urban, rural, and others. The essence of successfully working with these populations is that staff understands and is capable of working with this endless diversity.

The secret to developing a staff that is tolerant and understanding begins with recruitment, continues through training, is maintained through a strong culture of forbearance, and ends—or begins again—with leadership. As managers and administrators, we must be prepared to lead.

As an African-American director of the Ohio Department of Rehabilitation and Correction, a very large state correctional agency, this author has managed problems driven by intolerance and insensitivity on numerous occasions. Our most traumatic event happened on April 11, 1993 at the maximum-security Southern Ohio Correctional Facility. During an eleven-day riot, nine inmates and one officer were killed, and an entire wing of the prison was looted and destroyed. This siege resulted in eight formal fact-finding investigations. Most of the ensuing reports pointed out that the facility employees were doing "all the right things" on the surface; however, a simmering undercurrent of animosity existed between the mostly white Appalachian staff and the primarily urban, black prison population. The recommendations emerging from the reports, although not exclusively so, were to enhance cultural diversity training, foster respect for less common religions, and increase the diversity of institutional staff.

A 1994 Department of Rehabilitation and Correction report following the riot entitled "Erasing Racism," faced the problem head-on:

The Ohio Department of Rehabilitation and Correction acknowledges that racism exists in the Department as it does in society. Some effects of racism are conditions exclusive to the Department. Over 50 percent of inmates are minorities, while 20 percent of employees are minorities. Many institutions are located in rural areas with a low minority population (e.g. SOCF). Many inmates come from urban areas with large minority populations. The Department realizes that these differences often reflect cultural biases that can negatively affect inmate and staff relations. We also acknowledge the effect on staff-to-staff relations as we continue to increase minority employment. Given these realities, the Department is even more determined to erase racism from all aspects of departmental operations and prison life.

With previous efforts, and the emphasis of the aforementioned works, the Department of Rehabilitation and Correction began an intensive effort to recruit, assess, train, promote, and retain a more diverse workforce. There was also a major effort to minimize nepotism and to increase the education level of existing staff.

Recruitment

The most important resource of any organization is its staff. Attracting and retaining a talented group of diverse corrections professionals is a top priority. The department has worked diligently to recruit a diverse workforce. It is critical that as a department, we maintain our sensitivity when it comes to ensuring that the racial make-up of our staff is not out of kilter with the prison population that we supervise.

The unique Ohio Corrections Assessment Center began accepting corrections officer applications in December 1993. The Ohio Corrections Assessment Center recruits, assesses, and selects corrections officer applicants for all corrections officer positions statewide. This means the individual prisons no longer hire corrections officers directly. The Ohio Corrections Assessment Center includes a strong centralized recruitment component and provides a fair and equal opportunity for all applicants. The centralized location provides a better forum for targeting minority and female corrections officers to be placed within institutions composed of minimal minority staff. As of March 1997, the Ohio Corrections Assessment Center placed more than 4,300 corrections officers, including 28 percent who were minorities and 33 percent who were female staff. We must continue to strive toward meeting our diversity goals.

A recent successful improvement within the assessment process of the Ohio Corrections Assessment Center has been the addition of a behavioral response video test. Each person who applies for a corrections officer position must complete a sixty-six question video test to measure the applicant's behavioral response to correctional situations.

The test focuses on thirteen of the twenty-one knowledge, skills, and abilities deemed necessary for a corrections officer position. The test is composed of scenarios observed within a correctional setting, with the primary question for each scenario being "What should the officer do?" The goal is to solicit the applicant's initial response. It also serves as an educational tool in showing the applicants the ordinary demands of the work environment.

In addition to measuring an applicant's behavioral response, some of the scenarios require the applicant to read and apply statements of policy. None of the questions or answers is spoken in the video and the applicant must be able to read the questions and answers. The video test is administered on individual computers. All answers are scored four different ways to measure the identified aspects. Applicants must score 70 percent on the test, but there are also questions that are considered fatal errors and fail the applicant if selected. The test is also scored separately for emotional stability and reliance on back up. Preliminary data shows promise of a significant reduction in the first year turnover rate for corrections officers.

Through conscientious effort within the last twenty years, we have continually increased the percentage of minority employees throughout the department. While the Department of Rehabilitation and Correction is strongly committed to employing a diversified workforce, we want to be sure to also maintain a good balance. The long-term goal is that diversity is no longer an issue and becomes solely an appreciated value for all employees.

The Department of Rehabilitation and Correction strives to have at least one minority manager in every prison. This includes the wardens, deputy wardens, and the major. Of course, the result is often higher than a single minority manager. Furthermore, the Department of Rehabilitation and Correction employs a significant percentage of female managers in our correctional facilities as well. Therefore, whether we recruit new staff for entry-level positions or cultivate existing staff for vacant leadership positions, the mission of having a diverse staff is the same.

Training

As with most correctional agencies, the Department of Rehabilitation and Correction employees begin their careers with pre-service training. This training consists of a four-week curriculum for noncustody and a five-week course for custody staff. Several weeks of on-the-job training also precede employees working on their own. The diversity training during preservice introduces new employees to the many types of people, both staff and offender, with whom they will be working. Issues such as bias, assumptions, stereotypes, and values are addressed and discussed. Mandatory annual inservice training also includes a segment on diversity awareness.

Employees working with special populations, such as the elderly, youthful, and mentally impaired offenders, receive specialized sensitivity training. An example of a successful "culture" can be found at the Hocking Correctional Facility, a prison for elderly inmates. Hocking Correctional Facility staff quickly explain to new employees, especially those transferring from other prisons, that the Hocking Correctional Facility inmates have "special needs." The staff understand when an inmate does not comply with a direct order he could be suffering from deafness or senility, and not purposefully disobeying the order.

Similarly, employees working in residential treatment units for inmates with mental illness learn to recognize the difference between "acting out" and a manifestation of hallucinations or medication withdrawal. In both instances, custody staff work closely with medical employees. It is imperative that line staff through mid-management, to management and executive levels demonstrate "tolerance." Failure at any level leads to failure in the culture itself.

Employees selected for leadership positions receive more sophisticated training in diversity, which includes self-analysis and learning about management and the problems that may emerge among a diverse staff. One of the most interesting courses involves generational management. For example, many "baby boomers" are surprised to learn that "Gen Xers" are not lazy and disloyal, but rather, have different priorities than do the "boomers." Although they may not plan on life-long careers, they have a great deal to offer an organization.

Retention

It is crucial that as a department we not only attract diverse corrections professionals, but that we continue to retain our diversified workforce. The list of benefits that organizations are now able to offer to staff is compelling. It is extremely important to also create a culture that fosters an environment where people want to work and want to remain. The Department of Rehabilitation and Correction seeks to promote a balance between work and family life and to simultaneously help all employees realize their full potential. We have developed a wide range of programs to improve morale and influence and enhance professional development, personal growth, and communication skills while embracing diversity.

Some of the programs that organizations can offer include alternative work schedules and options. This program was created to explore the possibility of nontraditional and flexible work environments and schedules to meet the needs of our changing workforce and working families. Alternative work schedules and options are a definite plus to the recruitment and retention of dedicated employees. Slight adjustments such as flextime can result in dramatic boosts in productivity and job performance. Of course, some positions are more amenable to flexed schedules than others.

Women's coordinators assist female employees by providing information on educational and training opportunities and by offering support to encourage personal growth and professional advancement. The women's coordinators serve as a "voice" for female employees throughout the department. Through this juncture, women are able to bring concerns and issues to the attention of the administration. The administration may communicate various messages to female staff via their infrastructure.

Promotion

While it is an agency priority to recruit the best applicants, it is very critical to also have hiring practices in place to ensure that a diverse workforce is maintained. The Department of Rehabilitation and Correction has implemented a screening and interviewing committee policy to establish a standard procedure for the designation of individuals to serve on screening and interviewing committees that applies to all vacant positions within the department. Screening and interviewing committees must be comprised of male and female members, as well as minority and nonminority members, and are required to have a total of three members.

A learning organization is one that allows its employees the opportunity to grow within the organization. One of the many ways the Department of Rehabilitation and Correction strives to assist employees in their career goals is through tuition reimbursement. The Department of Rehabilitation and Correction recognizes the importance of educational development of our staff. In December 2000, the department began a tuition-reimbursement program for eligible, full-time permanent exempt employees. With an effective tuition-reimbursement program, the Department of Rehabilitation and Correction encourages career growth, promotes educational development, and provides parity with other educational programs offered for bargaining unit and exempt employees.

Another method of assisting employees with career advancement is through the Professional Alliance of Correctional Employees (PACE). This group organizes mentor/protégé relationships for staff, which normally evolves into a "shadowing" experience. PACE also conducts motivational and developmental training conferences for those employees interested in promotional opportunities and learning more about the department. In 1992, PACE began as the Female Issues Support Group, but the vision was clearly a focus on staff diversity. So, not only did the name change, but there was an expansion of the mission as well.

Leadership

Most agencies support offices such as Equal Employment Opportunity, Affirmative Action, and Standards of Employee Conduct that discourage discrimination and encourage equitable treatment among all employees. However, all these offices are no more than a veneer unless department leaders fully and publicly support them. It is a travesty at best to not know the laws governing equal opportunity for any employer.

Beyond tolerance and acceptance come support and celebration of our differences. Most prisons began this evolution with permission given for Black History Month informational outlets. These efforts led to recognition and celebrations of other cultures as well. In other words, it is good to acknowledge our differences—but to appreciate them is the real goal.

Ohio recently began noting an influx of Hispanic/Latino workers in several of our major cities. As those populations grow, so will the number of Latino offenders and the need for Hispanic staff. In anticipation of that need, the Department of Rehabilitation and Correction developed the Hispanic/Latino Committee, dedicated to improving the quality of life for Hispanic offenders and staff alike. The committee now boasts recruiters, a newsletter, an intranet website, and a host of available translators across the state. Employees involved with the committee hold recruitment drives in Hispanic churches and communities. Several have planned celebrations featuring speakers, films, cuisine, and education for Latin holidays and customs, providing a benchmark for institutions across the state.

Another important aspect of diversifying the face of corrections is to invite partnerships that serve to convey the message of tolerance and acceptance. These include volunteer groups, guest speakers, cultural celebrations, and most especially, the inclusion of minority religious leaders in the culture of institution and parole life. With our current emphasis on successful reentry, the black churches hold great promise as one-on-one resources for newly released offenders. In addition, organizations such as the Urban League and the NAACP support this philosophy.

Organizations such as the National Association for Blacks in Criminal Justice provide a great many resources for developing an agency that reflects a culture of diversity. Supporting women in corrections' conferences are also an excellent resource.

Perhaps the most effective way to reach staff with the message of diversity is to practice what you preach. Hire and promote diverse people in management positions. Publicize success stories. Encourage teamwork involving staff of all ages, races, and experience. The best way to "erase racism" is to illustrate to each and every employee, that we all have value. When a person of one culture is teamed with a person of a different culture, and they solve a problem together, they will recognize that all of us offer contributions toward our mutual success.

There is nothing mystical about having a diverse workforce. "Diversity" should not be a concept to be avoided. This author's experience is that when we admit our shortfalls and develop plans to address them, future problems are minimized. The mere size of correctional agencies dictate that problems will arise. Not tackling them in a forthright fashion can be as much of an issue as having a homogenous workforce.

Different parts of America, and even within various jurisdictions, require different strategies for diversity in terms of staff composition and programming. Nevertheless, in Ohio, the mission is, "just do the right thing." This is probably good advice for any correctional agency.

Chapter 11 Correctional Officers Need Cultural Diversity Training

Portia Hunt, Ph.D.
Professor, Counseling Psychology
Temple University
Philadelphia, Pennsylvania

Introduction

Correctional organizations are now experiencing and increasingly will continue to experience new changes in the workforce and environment. These changes will reverberate through the structure of work, labor relations, and the interface between technology and social systems. With the emergence of a more diverse employee base and increased reliance on computers to manage inmates, professional correctional staff will need to acquire more effective supervisory techniques.

Challenges to management will include helping staff gain competence in managing new technology and learning to work well with each other. To do this, supervisors themselves must become more culturally competent and technologically literate. At minimum, they will need training in the following things:

- Communications
- Conflict management
- Team building to restructure what their employees do and how they do it

This chapter describes the interpersonal problems that occur when a prison culture comes together with racially diverse minority cultures. The author examines some of the cultural and communication dynamics that supervisors and newly hired correctional officers need to understand to start the process of learning how to be culturally competent with African-Americans, European-Americans, and women from all cultural and ethnic groups. The main goals are to describe broad employment trends in the field, highlight specific cultural/gender conflicts between supervisors and minority correctional officers, and address work-related stress factors for professional women and minorities who are correctional officers. Obviously, if other ethnic and cultural groups are in the workforce or as inmates, it is imperative that managers learn how to deal effectively with these differences as well.

General Trends Affecting Correctional Institutions

The American workforce and organizations in it are changing rapidly. In the near future, the structure of work will be more complex and the employees will be different (Johnson and Packer, 1987). As a result of these trends, supervisors must learn how to develop productive work teams, reduce job-related stress, and retain satisfied workers.

Currently, the following trends are having an impact on the correctional workforce:

- Movement toward privatization of prisons
- Introduction of newer surveillance technology
- Shifts in workforce demographics
- Imposition of standards by outside professional organizations

The movement toward privatization of prisons is a catalyst for changing how the corrections business is run. Some private business results appear to prove their claim that they can do a better job than government with less money and more profit. Thus, such privatized facilities are increasing. Nonprivatized institutions have been forced to become more competitive to retain qualified employees and reduce losses associated with recruiting and training replacements. This has translated into more opportunities for women and minority correctional officers and greater challenges for institutions to create a work environment where these employees can earn a decent wage, have job security, and be respected for their contributions.

The introduction of newer surveillance technology to monitor, control, and secure prisons has changed the way visitors and inmates are processed. Training correctional officers to operate and deploy this new technology introduces a different type of dynamics between supervisors and employees than before. Technological skill will equalize employee opportunities in such a way that preferential treatment in the "good ol' boy" system may soon be obsolete. Adding diversity to the formula will mean that women and minorities will enter a more level playing field, where advancement will be based on knowledge and performance more than connections or seniority. Those with the advantage will be those who know how to use the new technology.

In the near future, shortages in the traditional employee base will cause a shift in labor demographics. This will result in an increase in the numbers of ethnic minorities and women, compared to the number of white male prison employees (Chaiken, 1995). With more diversity comes greater complexity. Women and minorities will import their cultural experiences and differences to the workplace. Therefore, managers will need to be prepared to face these changes and the challenges that they could bring as the new population grows to form a critical mass.

Adoption of a code of ethics and industry standards by professional criminal justice organizations raises the bar for performance and behavior in the workplace. These new standards should eradicate abusive practices in correctional institutions and significantly reduce discrimination and unprofessional behavior of supervisors and coworkers. Later in the chapter, we will discuss some of the recent standards that will compel correctional managers to change the way employees and inmates are handled.

Demographic Trends: Women and Minorities in Corrections

Demographic trends indicate there will be a rapid increase in minority populations in the United States over the next few decades. These changes are beginning to be reflected in corrections. For example, Table 1 shows that there were 418,248 correctional personnel in the United States in 2001 compared to 403,554 in 2000. In one short year, employees increased by 14,694 (American Correctional Association, 2001 and 2002).

The statistics in Table 1 also show that, while whites outnumber all ethnic groups combined and men outnumber women, the largest increase in nonwhite ethnic groups was among the Latino and Asian-American groups. In the next year, there were fewer black employees, about 2,000 less for both men and women. The trend in the increase of women officers was also borne out by another study, which showed that in 1991, women were 26 percent of the correctional officer workforce but 34 percent as of 2000 (Camp and Camp, 2000).

The expected influx of more varied ethnic groups and women into the ranks of correctional officers and supervisors will lead to changes in the prison culture and in the ability of these institutions to effectively administer to more diverse needs and deal with less familiar cultural mixes.

Table 2 shows additional trends on diversity and differences based on geography. It shows that in many states, white male correctional officers outnumber white women two to one. This is especially the case in the southern states. White males dominate the correctional officers' workforce based on total numbers of all racial groups except in Alabama, Arkansas, Mississippi, and South Carolina. Black males are in the majority in Alabama and hold a slight lead in South Carolina, and black females are in the majority in Mississippi, and hold a slight lead in Arkansas.

130

Table 1: State Correctional Employees by Race and Gender 2000-2001

	Males		Increase/ Decrease	Females		Increase/ Decrease
	2000	2001		2000	2001	
Whites	187,574	192,343	>	82,058	84,883	>
Blacks	42,852	40,289	<	38,325	36,121	<
Latino	19,545	22,534	>	8,768	10,180	>
Others *	8,607	9,326	>	4,826	5,475	>

* Refers to Asian Pacific and Native American employees

Source: American Correctional Association, 2001 and 2002

Table 2: Correctional Officers in Adult Prisons – Southern States by Race and Gender 2001

	Whites		Blacks		Latino		Others (Asian-American and Native American)	
	M	F	M	F	M	F	M	F
AL	872	53	1,142	394	0	0	13	1
AR	706	293	667	806	2	3	2	2
FL	7,867	2,505	2,016	1,859	523	105	155	44
GA	2,884	1,030	2,663	2,225	48	17	33	28
KY	1,113	369	60	30	6	1	4	3
LA	1,660	922	980	1,022	0	0	18	4
MD	2,298	262	1,394	1,348	20	0	18	4
MS	191	133	603	1,220	0	0	4	3
NC	NO DATA							
SC	785	303	1,402	1,193	0	0	33	18
TN	1,746	578	381	325	0	0	69	29
VA	2,429	555	1,764	1,613	51	15	3	12
WV	NO DATA							

Source: American Correctional Association, 2002

Although white men dominate correctional personnel in numbers and power at the state levels, the personnel statistics are going to change gradually over the next twenty years, especially with regard to an influx of Latinos and Asian-Americans. More women and persons of color will enter the correctional workforce; consequently, some of the existing behaviors and norms put in place by a white male-dominated workforce will have to change. These changes may bring about more conflicts, challenges, and new opportunities.

The potential for staff conflicts among blacks and whites, and males and females, is probably greatest in the South, with its history of a strained racial climate and traditional views toward females. Corrections administrators and supervisors will have the unique opportunity to convert conflict to challenges and challenges into caring and supportive working environments.

Studies show that states on the water borders of the United States or agricultural areas that hire seasonal workers from Central or South America will experience a large influx of detainees. As Table 3 illustrates, however, currently the majority of the correctional officers in these states—with the exception of New Mexico—are white males and females.

To handle the language differences effectively and deal with the related health, legal, and social problems of these immigrants, refugees, and the like, institutions in these states should employ a larger number of correctional workers from the same ethnic groups as the inmate population. In so doing, they also must provide leadership and training that creates a workplace that is fair and inclusive.

Inmate Population

While the total inmate population for both men and women declined slightly between 2000-2001, black males still represent the highest numbers, with Latino males increasing over the last two years (American Correctional Association, 2002). The increase in Latino inmates seems to be consistent with the increase of Latino personnel in

Table 3: Correctional Officers in Adult Corrections in Border States by Race and Gender

	Whites		Blacks		Latino		Others (Asian-American and Native American)	
	M	F	M	F	M	F	M	F
AZ	2,936	1,008	294	95	1,420	421	136	62
CA	13,455	3,098	3,317	1,639	7,063	1,810	1,817	347
DE	849	141	442	212	27	3	20	2
FL	7,867	2,505	2,016	1,859	523	105	155	441
NJ	3,491	263	1,716	370	470	63	49	5
NM	294	23	29	3	643	43	43	12
NY	17,814	978	1,469	769	643	125	156	38
PA	6,853	527	629	198	90	12	18	4
TX	8,013	3,779	2,839	3,694	3,208	1,196	147	73
WA	1,817	492	63	44	127	18	99	30

Source: American Correctional Association, 2002

Table 4: Inmate Population by Race and Gender 2000-2001

	Males		Increase/ Decrease	Females		Increase/ Decrease
	2000	2001		2000	2001	
Whites	401,245	383,346	<	52,210	30,918	<
Blacks	516,729	475,409	<	33,796	30,325	<
Latino	160,522	161,397	>	7,908	7,390	<
Others *	27,169	25,683	<	2,345	1,964	<

* Refers to Asian Pacific and Native American employees

Source: American Correctional Association, 2001 and 2002

Table 1. It may be that the need for bilingual personnel reflects the increase. However, it is interesting to note that black males remain the largest inmate population, yet black male personnel experienced the largest decrease of personnel. It is also clear that prison management continues to be dominated by whites and males.

The military and inmate subculture strongly influence the way supervisors and officers treat newcomers. It is this combined subculture that generates racial and gender stereotypes that foster a hostile climate leading to intense interpersonal stress for minority correctional officers. The supervisor sets a negative tone by ignoring unprofessional behavior between officers in the prison culture. Demographic changes in the workforce and in the inmate population will serve as a catalyst for prison management to reevaluate existing employee practices and develop a more flexible way of orienting new correctional officers from diverse backgrounds.

Prison Work Culture

Historically, the organizational culture of correctional facilities is male and white (European-American male) dominated. As a nation, our public institutions are generally hierarchical, linear, and formal. American white males developed the template for the structure of organizations. The policies, procedures, practices, and resources are structured similarly in all major institutions. The prison values, beliefs, and attitudes about right and wrong, good and bad, are the core beliefs of American organizations. The prison culture replicates American social structure (with racist beliefs embedded in its fiber).

Prisons develop their formal employee practices from military and the civil service culture. The informal culture in prisons comes from a mixture of street culture and inmate survival tactics.

Since the prison work culture is modeled after the military, it does not tolerate conflict or deviation from the social order. One is expected to conform and blindly adhere to rules. While on the surface, new correctional officers were formally prepared to follow the rules, beneath the formality and veneer, senior correctional officers used an informal method of orienting them. They used a combination of boot camp strategy, street vernacular, and strong-arm tactics to gain power and maintain the existing work hierarchy. To be a part of the in-group, new officers were expected to use force, verbal intimidation, and racist/sexist stereotypes to keep each other and inmates in line.

For example, in our immediate past, many saw women as weaker and blacks as inferior and violent. In unreformed prison systems today, seasoned correctional officers still use racial and gender stereotypes towards each other and with inmates to gain respect. These stereotypes reinforced the American patriarchal social order with men in charge and on top and women and minorities on the bottom. Many of the institutional practices were a blend of racism, sexism, and class superiority expressed together.

Currently, the challenge for correctional leadership is to insure that all correctional officers develop the interpersonal skills necessary for working effectively in racially mixed prisons with correctional officers from diverse backgrounds. While the history of the prison workforce has always had, to some extent, employees from different racial/gender groups (clerical, maintenance, social service, and food service), the communication problems among correctional officers often have been ignored or minimized.

Correctional leadership needs to be proactive in developing pathways for correctional officers to become culturally competent in work with minorities and women coworkers.

Cultural Encapsulation: Majority Identity Development

White correctional officers are likely to be culturally unaware of the way their cultural heritage influences they way they interact with minorities and women. According to research on white racial identity development, most whites do not see the need to discuss or explore their own racial attitudes and beliefs toward their own racial group (Helms, 1991). The same can be said for men, regardless of race. The lack of self-awareness and avoidance of one's majority group status may lead to further cultural encapsulation.

In male-dominated workplaces, the perspectives of nonwhites and women are usually disregarded. Although prison systems are rigidly structured to maintain control and safety, the adjustment for administrative assistants and women is not as smooth as it is for males in general and whites in particular. Cultural diversity training is needed to give voice to the unique perspectives and experiences of minorities and women who work at all levels in corrections.

Whites and males in supervisory roles may believe that standards for behavior are colorblind, gender-blind, and fairly applied to all without regard to race or gender. Fairness in a white-male dominated institution means that everyone is treated the same way under the same conditions regardless of life experience, sociopolitical context, and the collective treatment of exclusion. Their beliefs about fairness would work perfectly, if all ethnic group members shared only one cultural context, where the privileges, opportunities, and interpretation of language were the same. But, in reality, this is not true.

Color-blindness and gender-blindness assumes that people are not influenced by their sociopolitical history and that work-related interactions are experienced in an emotionally neutral context. Standards for behavior and interpretation of information are viewed differently depending on the specific ethnic group in question. African-Americans intuitively understand their two cultures' experiences, one within their own group and the other as a black group in white America. Unlike their counterparts, white Americans are marginally aware of their own cultural programming and superficially aware of others. When supervisors promote the myth of colorblindness, gender equity, and social class equity, they inadvertently are dismissing the socio-political history of white-male domination over various groups.

For diversity initiatives to succeed, whites and males in the prison workforce must learn about the ways they maintain the status quo by using race and gender dynamics to maintain a dysfunctional form of power over women and minorities. Since whites and males are not conscious of and naïve about their own cultural programming, they only can aspire to be superficially aware of others. Breaking the chains of cultural encapsulation is a hurdle that supervisors and leaders must confront if they are to be successful in creating an inclusive workforce with diverse employees.

The Hazing: Inclusion of Women and Minorities as Corrections Officers

All new officers receive a similar orientation to the formal rules in prisons. On paper, procedures are consistent. Supervisors have a major function of preparing and orienting new officers to the prison culture. They set the tone for the work climate. When problems arise, corrections officers are trained in reporting discrepancies and documenting their behavior. As was mentioned previously, informally, supervisors orient new employees through the use of boot camp practices, street language, and ethnic stereotypes. The supervisors'/coworkers' motivation is to force the officer to develop allegiance to authority, build toughness, and survive in a prison environment.

Many supervisors and senior officers believe that individuals must surrender their allegiance to their ethnic identity to prove their toughness. A type of hazing takes place, where the "old timers" test the new employees. Informal hazing tactics are used to teach adherence to the military hierarchy while simultaneously reinforcing racist and sexist stereotypes.

Blacks and women experience split loyalty to the job and to their ethnic identity status (race and gender). A study of the history of the prison workforce will show employees from different racial and gender groups; yet, the interpersonal conflicts and hazing often have been played down. The "old timers" will expect the new employees to transcend their cultural identity and develop loyalty to their jobs (Van Voorhis et al., 1991).

When women and minorities joined the ranks in smaller numbers, the old stereotypes prevailed. For example, even today, correctional officers still report these type of comments among coworkers: "If you are a black woman correctional officer, then you must be gay, or if you are feminine, you must be looking for companionship among the inmates. Black and Latino men are sexually promiscuous, explosive, and stupid. White and Latino women are weak, dizzy, gay, and indecisive." While beliefs like these were commonly expressed among the old timers, they are still made today.

At work, women and minority correctional officers have to find informal ways to refute stereotypes and prejudicial thinking, while simultaneously working to be included as part of the group. This added pressure creates a double bind, which typically is not understood by majority status individuals (whites and males). However, as more women and minorities enter the ranks, those outdated ways of testing a newcomer's loyalty will be challenged and eventually eliminated. Diversity training can help in this process.

If supervisors do not comprehend the diversity issues, employee conflicts will continue to plague the system. These communication problems intensify when both groups (blacks and whites, men and women) operate on the assumptions that each understands the cultural context of the other's behavior and applies the same meaning to the other's words. Correctional officers in the workforce must become knowledgeable about their own cultural programming and that of other groups; and in so doing, they learn how to work effectively with coworkers from other ethnic groups. Not doing so results in loss of workers, wages, and time.

Workplace stress is the number one reason for high employee turnover among women and blacks. The work climate is an important concern for administrators and supervisors to address as the prison population grows and as disgruntled employees exit in large numbers. While sexual bias against women is acknowledged, unintentional racism and ethnocentric bias toward minorities often is denied or minimized.

Diversity and Work-related Stress: How Supervisors Create Hell

Every few months or so, this author receives calls from the state employee assistance program with referrals from disgruntled correctional officers in need of counseling, stress reduction, and anger management. Most often, the referrals are blacks and women correctional officers who complain about horrendous treatment they have received at the hands of unscrupulous and abusive supervisors. Their complaints are about poor treatment from superiors within their own racial group and from whites and males in authority. Charges of racism, name-calling, sexual inappropriateness, retaliation (for reporting problems) among staff and with inmates are the regular complaints. Supervisors (captains, lieutenants, and sergeants) reprimand correctional officers by assigning them to less desirable work shifts, poorly managed cell blocks, or with punitive supervisors, who are known for making work "a living hell" for subordinates.

The source of most unnecessary work stress for women and minorities in corrections results from the enforcement of capricious and often arbitrarily applied rules, which hide problems. When the supervisor has limited skills to analyze interpersonal conflicts in a cultural context, the tendency is to apply the "one size fits all" to minorities and women. This is one of the major reasons why leadership in adult corrections should require all employees to develop skills in cultural competence. The "one size fits all" model looks fair on the surface, but when working with individuals from different ethnic backgrounds, the delivery of a command from a superior may be received very differently depending on both parties' ethnic backgrounds.

When African-Americans and whites work together, feelings about the power dynamics within a racial context usually influences the meta-message and interpretations of meaning. For example, a harsh forceful tone delivered by a white supervisor to a black officer could be interpreted as demeaning and racially motivated. Forceful commands in this mixed-race context will be seen with a different prism depending on the race, status, and communication style of the speaker and the listener.

Unfortunately, this cultural context is most often minimized by white supervisors and heightened by blacks. Pretending that these differences do not influence the way we communicate with each other is naïve. Supervisors and correctional officers have power struggles everyday in the workplace. When communications break down between a superior and a subordinate from different racial groups, the employee's reactions (if a minority group member) probably will intensify if racially loaded language is used. For example, if a white captain says to a black sergeant, "Boy, you better jump to it," the black officer may react differently than a white officer would.

Too many supervisors escalate interpersonal problems by communicating with subordinates in ways that evoke memories of discriminatory hatred directed at minorities and women. The end result is often employee-driven litigation, absenteeism, and frivolous disciplinary investigations. Too often, supervisors are instrumental in creating a hostile work climate that undermines the kind of cooperation they need to run a smooth operation. When supervisors ignore or minimize these types of incidents, their behavior costs the institution thousands of dollars.

Women, like minorities, end up experiencing unnecessary but debilitating work-related stress at the hands of poorly trained supervisors. Management needs to develop skills to prevent these kinds of stressful interactions. If the supervisors do not know the impact of their behavior within a racial and gender context, then the institution should require extensive work in communications training with supervising staff from different racial groups.

Some of the job-related stress could be ameliorated with better management practices, supervisory training, and most importantly, cultural diversity training. Many training directors and human resources departments try to address these problems by offering one cultural diversity session for three hours on political correctness and sensitivity toward minorities. These sessions are aimed at understanding what language triggers "the minority person" and teaching the group about racial strife. Self-examination of the majority persons' behavior is usually bypassed, or worst yet, ignored during the training. While well intentioned, this type of training barely touches the surface. This approach becomes a short-term Band-Aid that placates all groups. This sort of window dressing will serve to make problems worse.

To effectively address systemic issues of managing a diverse workforce in a multilayered organization, management must develop strategies to handle the multilayered interpersonal relationships. This includes being in touch with staff at all levels of the organization. The following suggestions are offered to help managers identify problems.

- Listen to complaints within the ranks and determine if a specific ethnic group is complaining about the same unfair treatment.
- Observe how supervisors follow policies and procedures. Look for indications of a match between the violation of a procedure and severity of discipline. Does the same violation receive similar reprimands for different racial group members?
- Select a training approach that infuses the professional aspects of prison culture, self-awareness of one's own ethnic identity, and illustrations of destructive/constructive interactions between supervisors and officers.
- Plan the intervention strategy that deals with real life work issues over a minimum of two years. Include a diverse group of correctional officers and supervisors in articulating the problems from each perspective.

Understanding cultural diversity in a prison contexts means that leadership not only values and understands other ethnic groups, but it includes understanding your own. In doing so, managers learn how to value, develop, and manage the complexity inherent in this diversity. As the prison culture includes more diverse employees, the potential for staff conflict will increase. Managing, translating, and resolving conflicts within an employee's cultural context within the prison culture will become an important task for correctional supervisors in the future. Cultural competence will soon be one of the professional standards for all employees in corrections.

Cultural Competence and Professional Standards

The American Correctional Association (ACA) is one of several organizations that set standards under which the profession operates. Its guiding principles include humanity, justice, protection, opportunity, knowledge, competence, and accountability. The American Correction-al Association's Code of Ethics was adopted by the Board of Governors and Delegate Assembly in 1994. This monumental achievement is the foundation for improvement of the profession and articulates what are each individual's areas of responsibility. Supervisors and officers are responsible to each other and the profession. This includes respect for coworkers and staff.

ACA has several mandates: to monitor, educate, and accredit prisons. One of the standards addresses improving the quality of services and promoting respect among professional correctional officers, offenders, and public stakeholders. It has developed courses to train future employees and provide continuing education for those in the field. The organization collects yearly statistics on personnel trends, the inmate population, turnover rates, and inmate violence. The data helps track trends and forecast future needs. While their standards are clear and impressive, the area of cultural competence is implied but not directly addressed.

What does the professional staff need to know about cultural competence process? This author believes that curiosity, awareness, and knowledge about one's own culture and others is an important beginning. Communications and conflict in the workplace requires that the manager/supervisor knows how to assess problems and help workers resolve them in a productive way. Understanding the meaning behind a communication within a cultural context is an important skill for professionals in corrections.

The next section in this chapter focuses on communication styles of two racial ethnic groups (blacks and whites) and gender differences. The objective is to illustrate how the cultural group's attitudes about persons influences how they interpret the behavior and verbal style of a person from a different cultural group. The different styles of communicating are closely linked to a person's cultural background. The reader is asked to use the information below as a general description of a group's cultural differences and not as a specific description of individual differences. The descriptions should not be used to stereotype a person or a group, but it should be used as a foundation for helping professionals unravel miscommunications between two different groups.

Communication Style Differences between African-American and European-American Correctional Officers

Much has been written about the communications style differences between African-Americans and European-Americans (Kochman, 1984) in everyday conversations. However, stylistic differences have not been written about extensively in the correctional literature (Hunt, 1993) because the field has not recognized the interplay between ethnic socialization patterns and interpretation of language in conversations. Stated differently, most people assume that all groups interpret language, meaning, and behavior through the same prism. Ethnically derived behaviors usually are ignored and or minimized in everyday conversations because we assume they are unimportant in the communication process. This assumption has resulted in miscommunication across different racial groups.

In correctional settings, poor communication is a major source of problems for staff and supervisors. Culturally competent staff needs to learn about different communication styles within a cultural context.

Below are several stylistic differences between blacks and whites that can occur in cross-racial communications. These groups were chosen because they represent the largest numbers of the racial mix of correctional personnel; they have reached a critical mass of race and gender diversity in the workplace; and they have experienced enormous work-related stress in corrections. This stress is a microcosm of lower status groups in the United States and as such, they are often the recipients of verbal harassment. The reader is warned to think of the descriptions below as general styles and not characteristic of all individuals in any racial/gender groups. Group styles are shared but do not necessarily reflect the range and totality of any individual regardless of race or gender. Individuals who are culturally competent understand this distinction and will not use this information to pigeonhole a person from any racial group.

Emotional Expressiveness

Heightened emotional expressiveness is a core communication style among African-Americans (Kochman, 1984). It is evident in behavior, conversation, demeanor, attitudes, and worldview. When African-Americans talk to each other, the conversation is often intense, active, quick, and ritualistic. The conversational tone is heightened to persuade the listener. For African-Americans, persuasion in conversation is extremely important. The speaker's voice, tone, volume, exaggerated nonverbal gestures, and repetition of key points strengthens persuasion. How the person says it is as important as what a speaker says. There is a fine line between truth and belief. If what you say is deemed credible, how you say it convinces the listener. A speaker is believable when emphasis is given to creative poetic phrasing, expressive body movements, facial gestures, and a convincing argument based on real life testimonials.

While this style is characteristic of African-Americans as an ethnic group, it is not unique. In certain regions of the country, whites share similar styles. An example of this is white charismatic religious groups in southern states. Emotional presentation is used for persuasion. Also, other white ethnic groups, Italians, Jews, and certain Latino groups, have active communication styles. However, African-Americans generally are noted for their heightened emotional expressiveness.

Restrained emotional expressiveness is a core value among European-Americans. In conversations, European-Americans try to separate emotions from the message (Kochman, 1984). The intent is to let the message and not the emotions convince the listener. The conversational tone is often controlled, calm, and factual. The speaker's delivery is slower, sequential, deductive, and linear. What one says must not be influenced by emotion. There is a separation between truth and personal beliefs. How one says "it," especially if the speaker delivers the message in a nonemotional tone, is likely to persuade the listener. Facts and objective observations are valued over personal experience. Credibility is given to the speaker when information is conveyed in a dispassionate manner.

The exception to this rule can be seen in blue-collar occupations, which were predominately controlled by white ethnic minorities in unions. In the past, this included first and second generation Irish, Italians, and Polish immigrants. Emotional expressiveness was expected in lower social economic status groups. However, as more white ethnic individuals moved into middle management positions, emotional restraint became a shared value in the workplace.

Innocence or Guilt

How do you know if a person is lying or telling the truth? Direct eye contact and defending oneself by pleading one's case are signals European-Americans use to determine innocence. Breaking eye contact and silence are often taken as evidence of trying to hide something. These behaviors do not have the same meanings for African-Americans and European-Americans. Eye contact is viewed differently in situations where a person is called on to defend himself for an error or transgression. Making eye contact and explaining your innocence has different meaning for African-Americans and European-Americans. In fact, culturally determined behaviors are at the opposite end of the spectrum for these two ethnic groups.

This example can be seen in the way parents train their children. When accused of something, African-American children are taught to remain silent if they are innocent. Explaining your innocence is a sure sign of guilt. The general belief is, "If you didn't do it, then there's no need to explain." The general belief for an African-American parent is that talking too much is a sign of guilt. Parents expect children to look down and simply state, "I didn't do it." When innocent, the child also should show respect and deference by looking down. Sustaining direct eye contact with an authority figure is a sign of disrespect and arrogance. Directly starring may result in punishment. African-American parents tell children, "Don't roll your eyes at me." A direct stare in another's eye is a challenge to authority.

Making direct eye contact when accused is a sure sign of innocence for European-Americans. The American educational and justice systems are built on defending yourself when accused. Children are expected not only to make direct eye contact, they also must explain why they are innocent. Teachers will tell students, "If you didn't do it, look me in the eye and tell me why you didn't do it." Eye contact denotes believability, and self-defense is a sign of innocence.

Confronting the Accuser

On the other hand, if accused, an African-American expects to directly confront the accuser. The purpose is to correct or clarify the accusation. Since African-Americans are comfortable with expressing emotion, speaking directly to the accuser is not viewed as a challenge. The person expects the accuser to "tell me to my face." If the African-American norm is violated, as we shall see in the European-American context, the African-American employee will distrust supervisors and coworkers who are not open and direct. Person-to-person contact is a strong value for African-Americans, especially if they are being reported for problematic behavior.

For European-Americans, the opposite rule applies. If accused, the coworker expects the supervisor to confront the accused. One's job title or the position in the hierarchy guides European-Americans' approach when handling conflict. Since most workplaces are hierarchical, European-Americans expect supervisors to confront subordinates. For a European-American's coworker to directly confront another coworker violates the hierarchy. Coworkers of equal status do not have the authority to correct another coworker. To do so would violate the social order and potentially could invite conflict. Conflict is handled and resolved by the supervisor, the one in charge. To not do so brings about unnecessary interpersonal conflict between coworkers.

In addition, the European-American coworker expects the supervisor to conceal his or her identity. To not do so would be viewed as a hostile act against the accuser. If confronted directly by the coworker, the European-American accuser may believe that he or she is in danger. The European-Americans may respond to the African-Americans with silence or avoidance. If the supervisor reveals the accuser's identity, this may result in harassment charges.

These cultural stylistic differences are one of the greatest sources of workplace stress between African-Americans and European-Americans. Both groups will view the other's cultural style with distrust and suspicion. If the African-American employees are not allowed to speak directly with their accusers, they may conclude that a conspiracy is taking place and they are a target for termination. And, if the European-Americans are confronted directly, they may feel attacked and/or expect personal retaliation. For them, then, the workplace becomes a potentially hostile place.

Cues for Aggression: Movement versus Words

Triggers for physical aggression are another area where African-American and European-American signals vary depending in part by ethnically determined norms. Emotional expression, group influence, and movement govern African-Americans' behavior. Blacks will use ritualistic behavior in the form of challenges to fight, exaggerated insults, or threats to inhibit aggression especially in the presence of their peer group. The terms "slamming, woofing, and popping off" are examples of verbal challenges. Their peer group will incite the challengers to outwit each other. This teasing intensifies emotion and creates a protective boundary to defuse actual contact between the challengers. If the behavior occurs between two individuals without the group's presence, physical contact is likely to occur.

Verbal attacks are a part of posturing for blacks. The peer group regulates the social boundaries between challengers. Words are used to inhibit aggression. Movement toward one's opponent, on the other hand, is the trigger for fighting among blacks. Comments like "he put his finger in my face; he moved on me; he got in my space" are examples of movement. Blacks often interpret ambiguous movement in an argument as an invitation to fight. Physical contact usually occurs when one person makes a move toward the other. Whites may use movement to reduce distance and calm tension between each. Movement is interpreted differently between the two groups.

Among whites, words, not movement, are provocative. If a threat is spoken, whites assume one is going to act within a short time frame. Because European-Americans do not use a verbal posturing style to inhibit aggression, they often misread cues from African-Americans. And because European-Americans may use physical movement (holding hands in front of themselves to calm the other person down) to inhibit aggression, African-Americans may interpret them as being provocative. Emotional expressiveness, movement, and verbal threats have different meanings in each group's cultural context.

148

These different styles can have dire consequences for inmates and staff in a correctional setting. Consider the potential conflict between offenders from the same ethnic group being observed by an officer from a different ethnic group. The likelihood of misinterpreting others behaviors can lead to overreacting or underreacting based on ones cultural context.

Conversational Style Differences: A Comparison between Men and Women

Over the last two decades, social scientists have been observing sex-role differences between men and women (Gilligan 1982, Tannen, 1986) and their ways of viewing and understanding conversations. Although variability exists within each sex-role group, as it does for race, extensive research has revealed some relatively consistent differences that have an impact on the ways we relate to each other and interpret each other's behavior. Although often unconscious to us, sex-role communication is cross-cultural in nature. Misunderstandings occur frequently in everyday interactions and especially in the workplace. It is important for correctional officers and supervisors to understand sex-role styles, expectations, and implications, especially as they relate to hiring, retaining, and evaluating women in male-dominated occupations. This section briefly describes the different perspectives, conversational styles, implications, and harmful sex-role stereotypes in correctional settings.

Sex-role Perspectives

Men and women, from birth on, are raised in different ways that shape specific sex-role behaviors. Our cultural traditions are rooted in the notion of man being the hunter and woman being the gatherer. Men protect women and women protect children. Because of these socially derived functions, women tend to have different perspectives about relationships, power, and conflict. Boys are trained to be independent, autonomous, strong, and stern. Emphasis for men is on individuality, separateness, and competition—play to win at all cost. Emotions may be expressed only when angry and the goal is to beat out the opponent. If hurt, grin and bear it. Tough men don't cry.

Women, on the other hand, are taught to be interdependent, concerned for others, emotional, and responsible for preserving relationships. Emotional expression, close social relationships, sharing and togetherness, are important aspects of being a part of the human community. Relationships are emphasized over individuality. Competition and winning should not be sacrificed at the expense of the relationship. How one plays the game is as important as winning. Emotional expression is an intrinsic value. They may experience and express the entire range of sadness, tenderness, hurt, joy, love, and anger. Crying does not diminish one's strength. Release of emotions is important to maintain health. Women often are caught in a dilemma when working in corrections.

Because women have different perspectives, they enter conversations with different expectations. Men use language to set up rules, power relationships, and hierarchies and women use it to develop connections, share information, and work with teams. For men, flexing muscles and showing who is in charge of a group is important. Their communication style is direct, formal, and fact based.

Men understand the world in literal terms. Information is approached from a logical, analytical point of view. In leading, one must use force to maintain order. For women, talking problems through is important. Persuasion is preferred over force. Women generally do not want or need to flex their muscles to gain cooperation. They often are able to use intuition and logic to solve problems.

Since correctional settings are developed for men by men, women enter work from a one-down position. The prison organization is strictly ordered from top down, rules are fixed and directives are literal. For a woman entering this setting, she must play by the rules. As such, she will risk having her sexuality and sex-role status questioned by peers and supervisors. She may be accused of being too "masculine," a lesbian, or some other sex-role stereotype. If she's "too feminine," she may be accused to being too weak, too soft, or incompetent.

Because the male style is top down and power based, some researchers pose the question: does the male style increase inmate-officer attacks (Rowan, 1996)? Several researchers have observed, while just as firm as their male counterparts, female correctional officers have a calming effect on prisoners and tend to reduce prison violence (Jacob, 1983; Rowan, 1996).

Conversational Styles

Men and women talk differently to and with each other and, as a result, they have different expectations as a listener and as a speaker. Women focus on the meaning of a message as well as the message itself. Women look for cues when talking and men tend to listen for the literal meaning. Men are direct: "You should say exactly what you mean," while women are less direct: "You should know what I mean without me having to directly tell you."

An exaggerated example is a woman who says to her husband, "Would you like to stop and get something to eat?" The indirect meaning from the woman is, "I would like to stop and eat." A man might misread this request as having a choice and say, "No" and keep driving. At which point the woman may become annoyed because he ignored her request. The man's style is direct; he would say, "I want to stop and eat." Men often report feeling manipulated when women are indirect.

Women prefer the process of talking through problems before reaching decisions. They gather opinions from others, discuss them, weigh data, and reach independent conclusions with expanded information. Their process is interactive, reflective, open, and shared. Men, on the other hand, solve problems with little input from others. Their process is often closed and solitary. They arrive at conclusions by a reduction of data rather than expansion. Men interpret women's style as being inefficient, indecisive, and slow. Women see men as being exclusive, arbitrary, and narrow. Consider the potential for clashes of styles in prisons. The male style is preferred for most supervisors because the control of decisions is within the hands of one or two people and handed down to the rank and file.

While the male style may be more efficient, it results in officers covering their backs and working as independent units without accountability to the team. The correctional officers may blindly execute procedures without concern for later shifts. With more diverse workers, the need to build interlocking teams will become more important. Women are more skilled at team building. Their style tends to be inclusive and, as such, team members may be operating from the same information base.

A Call to the Profession: Develop Standards for Cultural Competence

One part of the ethical code of the American Correctional Association states that "Members shall maintain relationships with colleagues to promote mutual respect within the profession and improve the quality of service." Cultural diversity competency is not a requirement of correctional officers' education and training, but it is certainly needed and often overlooked in the field. Consequently, many officers enter the field believing that since we are all Americans, we are all the same.

While we share a commonality as human beings, all of us are a part of different groups, which shapes our beliefs and behaviors with others. We all belong to a racial and ethnic group; we all belong to a sex-role group; we all belong to a social class, a profession or trade, and we all live in a region of the United States that has its own linguistic patterns and ways of relating to others in that region. In other words, we all share multiple identities. The way correctional officers behave with each other in the workplace is a composite of the attitudes and values they bring with them from their cultural background, and from cross-racial interactions with others. Professional organizations must address these issues.

152

Racial and ethnic identity can be somewhat elusive because we usually do not think about it. When we share a common language, the uniqueness of our differences within our cultural upbringing is muted. However, our race and ethnic identity have a strong influence over our interpersonal behavior as shown in the earlier descriptions of general characteristics of groups. They were not intended to be inclusive of all individuals in those groups. Rather, they are group archetypes, and as such, the characteristics will vary among individuals within the same group. Other factors which also influence ethnic and sex-role behavior include regional characteristics, family values (what one learned in his or her family), social class status, education, occupation, and experiences with other racial groups. Our experiences as an ethnic group member in American culture are complex. However, our beliefs, behaviors, and the meanings that we attribute to others often result in miscommunication among culturally different people.

In correctional settings, misunderstandings among supervisors, coworkers, and inmates are a key source of stress for all employees. If the profession does not develop and clearly point the way for training supervisors and correctional officers, prison and jail workplaces will continue to breed chronic burnout, poor morale, physical distress, high job turnover, and absenteeism. This author and other correctional professionals believe that this profession can rise to the challenge and create the professional training standards needed for a diverse workforce.

References

American Correctional Association. 2001. *Directory of Adult and Juvenile Correctional Departments, Institutions, Agencies, and Probation and Parole Authorities.* Lanham, Maryland: American Correctional Association.

———. 2002. *Directory of Adult and Juvenile Correctional Departments, Institutions, Agencies, and Probation and Parole Authorities.* Lanham, Maryland: American Correctional Association.

Caggins, E. 1993. Multiculturalism in Corrections: Perceptions and Awareness. *In Understanding Cultural Diversity*. Lanham, Maryland: American Correctional Association.

Camp, C. G. and M. G. Camp. 2000. *The Corrections Yearbook 2000: Adult Corrections*. Middletown, Connecticut: Criminal Justice Institute, Inc.

Chaiken, Jan. 1995. *Census of State and Federal Correctional Facilities*. Washington, D.C.: U.S. Department of Justice, Bureau of Justice Statistics.

Curry, T. 1993. Diversity in the Workplace. In *Understanding Cultural Diversity*. Lanham, Maryland: American Correctional Association.

Finn, P. 2000. *Addressing Correctional Officer Stress: Programs and Strategies*. Washington, D.C.: National Institute of Justice.

Gilligan, C. 1982. *In a Different Voice*. Cambridge, Massachusetts: Harvard University Press.

Helms, J. E. 1990. *Black and White Racial Identity*. New York: Greenwood Press.

Hunt, P. L. 1993. Expression of African-American Culture in Corrections. In *Understanding Cultural Diversity*. Lanham, Maryland: American Correctional Association.

Hunt, P. L. and L. Golden. 1992. Racial Differences and the Supervision of Inmates. In *The Effective Correctional Officer*. Lanham, Maryland: American Correctional Association.

Jacob, J. B. 1983. *New Perspectives on Prison and Imprisonment*. Ithaca, New York: Cornell University Press.

Johnson, W. and A. Packer. 1987. *Workforce 2000: Work and Workers for the 21st Century*. Indianapolis: The Hudson Institute.

Kochman, T. 1984. *Black and White Styles in Conflict*. Chicago: University of Chicago Press.

Rowan, J. 1996. Who Is Safer in Male Maximum Security Prisons? *Corrections Today*. 52(5): 62-70.

Tannen, D. 1986. *That's Not What I Meant: How Conversational Style Makes or Breaks Your Relations with Others*. New York: William Morrow & Co.

Van Voorhis, P., F. Cullen, B. Link, and N. Wolfe. 1991. The Impact of Race and Sex-role on Correctional Officers' Orientation to the Integrated Environment. *Journal of Research in Crime and Delinquency*. 28(4): 472-500.

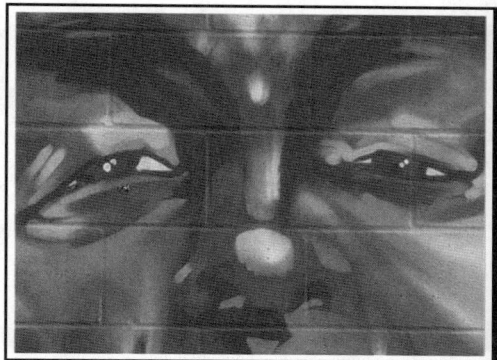

Index

B

C

generational diversity, 32

inmate population trends affecting
need for, 132-134

Latinos in corrections, 66-67, 73, 76

majority culture's unawareness,
136-137

organizational culture and, 134-135

orientation of new minority and
female corrections officers, 137-
139

professional standards, 142-143

punishment, used as form of, 2

religious diversity, 58

stress, work-related, 139-142

trends creating need for, 128-129

domestic violence amongst Latinas,
71-72

Duerk, Judith (Circle of Stones), 115-
116

E

Eastern religions, 54, 59, 95-96

Edmunds, Gayl R., 81-85, 159

emotional expressiveness, 144-145

emotional intelligence, 37, 47

employee shortages, 129

ethics codes

American Correctional Association
(ACA), vii-viii

development of, 129

eye contact, 145-146

F

feedback and generational communica-

tion styles, 41-42

importance of feedback, 44, 46-47

positive feedback, value of, 46-47

procedures for, 44-46

right time and place for, 42-43, 44-
46

sounding boards or interpreters,
generational, 40, 45-46, 47-48

training, 43, 44, 46

G

gender, see women in corrections

Generation X, 23-24, 25, 32, 39, 40-41,
42, 43, 47, 48-49

Generation Y, 25, 39, 40, 43, 47, 48-49

generational diversity, 11-29, 31-52, see
also specific generations

advantages of, 12, 24, 28-29

Asian-Americans, 96-97

broad definition of diversity, value
of, 32, 33-35, 51

conditions creating, 39-41

correctional careers, growth and
change in, 11, 15-18

current generational groups, 25, 39

feedback, see feedback and generational communication styles

inmate population and, 11, 15-16,
24-26, 50

sounding boards or interpreters,
generational, 40, 45-46, 47-48

standard generational breakdowns,
25, 39-40

stereotyping and assumptions, 12,

role models lacking for African-
American women in corrections,
105-106

S

self-understanding, 37
communication and diversity, 3, 6,
7-9
majority culture's unawareness of
gender and racial issues, 136-137
September 11 terrorist attacks, 57-58,
89, 90, 91
sexism and sex differences, *see* women
in corrections
shadowing, 20-22
Smalls, Carla J., viii-ix, 161
stereotyping and assumptions
American Indians, 82, 83, 84
Asian-Americans, 88-91
generational diversity, 12, 13-15, 48-
50
Latinos in corrections, 76-77
orientation of new minority and
female corrections officers, 137-
139
stress, work-related, 139-142
Sturgeon, William "Bill," 11-29, 161-162
surveillance technology, effect of
changes in, 129

T

training, 121-122, *see also* diversity
training
African-American women in correc-

tions, 105-106, 109-112, 113
baby boomers as correctional staff,
coming loss of, 19
classroom instruction, 19-20
feedback and generational diversity, 43, 44, 46
generational diversity, ensuring,
19-24
mentoring, 20
shadowing, 20-22
truth-telling/innocence vs. lying/guilt,
body language associated with,
145-146

V

valuing diversity and difference, 6, 33,
34, 35-37
variations, and differences within eth-
nic groups
American Indians, 83
Asian-Americans, 91-92, 94, 95-96
Latinos, 66, 76
"Veterans" generation ("The Greatest
Generation"), 25, 39, 40, 42, 46, 48
49
victims of crime
Latinas, 71-72
Latinos, 68-71

W

weapons qualification, 111
wholeness, diversity as sense of, 51-52
Wilkinson, Reginald A., 117-125, 162
women in corrections, 107, 137-139

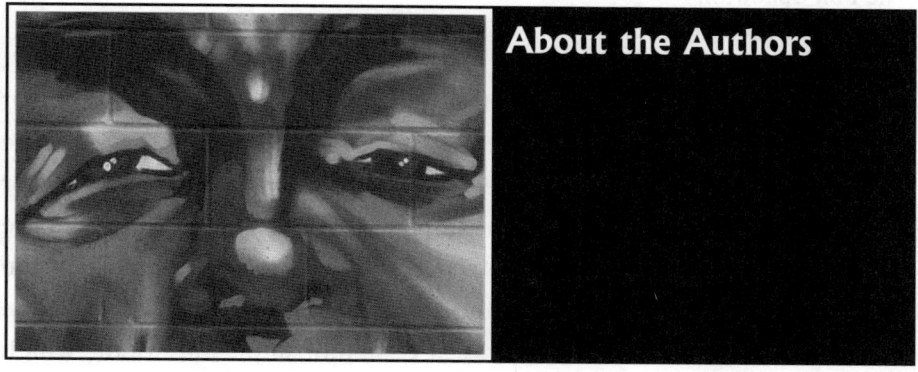

About the Authors

Ana T. Aguirre

Ana T. Aguirre, senior trainer with the Texas Juvenile Probation Commission (TJPC), was employed in Terry County for one year and Andrews County for nine years as assistant chief juvenile probation officer prior to joining the Texas Juvenile Probation Commission in 1992 as a program specialist and later a training specialist. Ms. Aguirre serves as the contact person regarding juvenile sex offender services and issues (supervision, assessment, registration, technical assistance) and as a resource on victim's services. She currently serves on the Texas Department of Criminal Justice Risk Assessment Review Committee (Sex Offender), the Texas Juvenile Probation Commission Sex Offender Management Program Team, and the Council on Sex Offender Treatment Interagency Committee. In addition, Ms. Aguirre serves as a consultant on the National Advisory Committee for the National Center on Sexual Behavior of Youth/Center on Child Abuse and Neglect out of the University of Oklahoma, an initiative funded by Office of Juvenile Justice and Delinquency Prevention. She has an Associate of Arts in Law Enforcement from South Plains College in Levelland, Texas, a Bachelor of Science in Criminal Justice from Southwest Texas State University in San Marcos, Texas, and a Master of Science in Criminal Justice Management from Sam Houston State University in Huntsville, Texas.

167

Raul Banasco

Warden Raul Banasco started his correctional law enforcement career in 1989 as a correctional officer. He held that position before moving up to the positions of correctional probation officer and senior correctional probation officer in the Classification Department. Some years later, Warden Banasco took on the challenge of classification supervisor and then was promoted to senior classification supervisor. In 1995, he was awarded the title of assistant superintendent, which was later renamed assistant warden. In 2003, he became the youngest and the first Hispanic (Cuban/Puerto Rican) warden in the Florida Department of Corrections' history.

Mary V. Leftridge Byrd

Mary V. Leftridge Byrd serves as deputy secretary with the Pennsylvania Department of Corrections. She is responsible for inmate programs, victim's services, community corrections, transition and reentry programs, and corrections education. She is also responsible for four state correctional institutions that house the system's two diagnostic centers, the two women's prisons, and the institution that provides intensive programs to address histories of severe alcohol and other drug addiction. She has served as superintendent or warden of four state correctional facilities in Pennsylvania and Maryland and has more than twenty-five years in corrections and human services. She offers particular expertise in working with female offenders, constituency building, corrections operations, and program implementation.

Bob Crouch

Bob Crouch is a correctional training instructor for the North Carolina Department of Corrections in Apex, North Carolina.

Linda A. Dillon

Linda A. Dillon retired from the Illinois Department of Corrections in 2003 as the chief of program services. She has more than twenty years of experience in corrections and more than ten years of direct community experience. She is now Chief Executive Officer/Consultant of Innovative Concepts in Springfield, Illinois. At the Illinois Department of Corrections, her areas of oversight included the agency's internal audit control process; medical and health care services; mental health and psychiatric services; addiction recovery management; sex offender management; dietary and nutritional services; educational and vocational services; library and college programs; victim services, and other programs or services which aid the offender as they return to the community until their point of discharge from parole. Ms. Dillon was appointed by the governor to serve on the following boards: the Sex Offender Management Board; the Mental Health Evaluation and Treatment Task Force Committee; the Governor's Advisory Council on Literacy; and the Juvenile Crime Advisory Task Force. She was also a committee member on the Inspector General's Task Force on Forensic Unit Security for the Illinois Department of Mental Heath. Ms. Dillon has a Master of Science in psychology with an emphasis in behavioral studies and general psychology (1982); Master of Arts in communication science with an emphasis in interpersonal communications (1978); and a Bachelor of Arts in behavioral studies with an emphasis in psychology and personal growth (1976).

Gayl R. Edmunds

Gayl R. Edmunds is the program director for the Indian Alcohol Treatment Service in Wichita, Kansas.

Portia L. Hunt, Ph.D.

Portia L. Hunt, Ph.D., a professor of counseling psychology at Temple University, currently serves as the program coordinator and director of the Bradley Counseling Psychology Clinic. She is responsible for training doctoral level students for working in an urban, multicultural context. As a licensed psychologist in the state of Pennsylvania, she has provided mental health services to state and local employees in corrections and law enforcement. She is also the president and founder of Eclipse Consultant Group, Inc., a firm that provides customized consultation and training in cultural diversity. She is nationally known as an expert in the fields of racial and ethnic identity, intercultural communication, and organization development and was appointed by the Office of Juvenile Justice and Delinquency Prevention's Special Emphasis Division to their State and Local Technical Assistance and Training Program. Dr Hunt's recent consultation projects include: faith-based diversity training for clergy and leaders in the Episcopal Diocese of Pennsylvania; diversity training for senior management, employees, and police and fire fighters for the city of Reading, Pennsylvania; and organizational development for management and staff of the Association of Pennsylvania State Colleges and University Faculty Union. She has achieved regional and national recognition as a dynamic and compelling speaker and trainer and has appeared frequently on television and radio in the Philadelphia area and on national television. The *Philadelphia Journal* also honored her as one of the 1995-1996 "Women to Watch." The Urban League of Philadelphia presented her with their Annual "The State of Black Philadelphia Award" in the early 90s for outstanding achievement and contribution to the community. She is the 2003 recipient of the Philadelphia Chapter of the NAACP Award to an Exemplary Citizen.

Meesim Lee

In her current capacity as the branch chief for management information services for the South Carolina Department of Corrections, Mrs. Lee supervises the development of an executive information system and research/statistics activities. She earned her B.A. and M.S. degrees in economics from the University of Hong Kong and started employment at South Carolina Department of Corrections in 1971, after furthering her graduate studies at the University of South Carolina. During her thirty-two-year tenure in corrections, she developed prison population projection models, provided technical and analytical support to the

South Carolina Sentencing Guidelines Commission, conducted statutory impact analyses, and oversaw automation projects in South Carolina Department of Corrections. She served as a principal investigator for a National Institute of Justice funded research project in 1998-2000 and provided technical assistance on behalf of the National Institute of Corrections in 2001.

Carla J. Smalls

Carla J. Smalls is a correctional program specialist with the Community Corrections Division of the National Institute of Corrections and is responsible for coordinating and delivering technical assistance to state and local community corrections agencies. She holds a Bachelor of Arts in sociology and a Master of Arts in community psychology from the University of South Carolina and has more than twenty-five years of experience in criminal justice in the areas of juvenile justice, adult probation and parole, and training. Ms. Smalls is an active member of the American Correctional Association (ACA) and the National Association of Blacks in Criminal Justice. She conducts training seminars on both the national and state levels. She has served on the ACA's Board of Governors, ACA's Delegate Assembly, and Program Planning Committee. She is also a founding member of the Association of Women Executives in Corrections.

William "Bill" Sturgeon

William "Bill" Sturgeon has more than twenty-five years of experience in the criminal justice field. An author, teacher, trainer, practitioner, expert witness, and internationally recognized criminal justice consultant, he has received numerous awards and commendations for his work. Mr. Sturgeon has been a consultant for the U.S. Department of Justice, the National Institute of Corrections for over twenty years in the areas of management, operations, training, security, and supervision. He has been a consultant for the federal, state, and county governments, as well as national and international corporations. He has served as a technical consultant for correctional training videos, and in 1995, he won a Telly Award for "Best Training" video in its class. He has also consulted abroad in the United Kingdom, the Netherlands, Haiti, and the Republic of South Africa. Mr. Sturgeon has written several articles and coauthored two books, *No Time to Play: Youthful Offenders in Adult Corrections*, and *Recess Is Over: Managing Youthful Offenders in Adult Systems*, both published by the American Correctional Association. He has a Bachelor of Science from Southern Vermont College and a Master of Arts in criminal justice administration from Goddard College. He received his training in mediation and conflict resolution from the Harvard School of Public Health. He is a decorated Vietnam veteran who served with the 101st Airborne Division.

Reginald A. Wilkinson, Ed.D.

Dr. Reginald A. Wilkinson is the director of the Ohio Department of Rehabilitation and Correction. He is also a past president of the American Correctional Association and a recipient of ACA's E. R. Cass Correctional Achievement Award. Director Wilkinson is the current president of the Association of State Correctional Administrators and vice chair for North America of the International Corrections and Prisons Association. He has more than thirty years of experience in corrections.

Doris Woodruff-Filbey

Doris Woodruff-Filbey, M.Div., is ordained in the Christian Church (Disciples of Christ). Prior to her retirement in 2002, she served as director of religious services and community involvement for the Indiana Department of Correction for eleven years. She also served as chaplain at the Indiana Women's Prison and the Indianapolis Juvenile Correctional Facility. Reverend Woodruff is the immediate past president of the American Correctional Chaplains Association and a certified member of the American Association of Pastoral Counselors (retired). She presently serves as a correctional consultant and is pursuing her interest in creative writing.